Who Am I, Really?

Who Am I, Really?

A Woman's Journey to God-Significance

DR. LYNDA HUNTER

WORD PUBLISHING
NASHVILLE
A Thomas Nelson Company

Published by Word Publishing, a Thomas Nelson, Inc., Company, P.O. Box 141000, Nashville, Tennessee 37214 in association with the literary agency of Alive Communications, Inc., 7680 Goddard Street, Suite 200, Colorado Springs, CO 80920.

Many of the names used in this book have been changed to protect the privacy of those individuals.

Library of Congress Cataloging-in-Publication Data

Hunter, Lynda.

Who am I, really? : a woman's journey to God-significance / Lynda Hunter.

p. cm.

ISBN 0-8499-4246-2 (tp)

1. Self-esteem—Religious aspects—Christianity. 2. Christian women—Religious life. 3. Self-esteem in women. I. Title.

BV4647.S43 H86 2001

248.8'43—dc21 2001017607

Printed in the United States of America

1 2 3 4 5 6 PHX 05 04 03 02 01

To every woman who has ever wondered *Who Am I?* May the words in this book replace the lie with the truth of God's love and your value through Him. And then, may you pass that truth on to those around you.

For Dave, my best friend and faithful companion, who shares the pain and the joy of discovering the moving still point of life.

Contents

…

Acknowledgments

My name appears on the cover as the author of this book, but many others helped it become a reality through their careful criticism, generous suggestions, and timely support. I'd like to say thank you to them from the bottom of my heart.

To Dave Bjorklund, my husband, best friend, and greatest cheerleader;
To my six children, whose student I become every day;
To Greg Johnson and his uncanny ability to see gold in the dross;
To Mark Sweeney and Debbie Wickwire, whose vision I greatly admire;
To Bridgett O'Lannerghty for her wise and gracious editorial guidance;
And to all those who generously allowed me to use their stories.

Introduction

"Once upon a time . . ."

We've heard the stories. She emerges from humble beginnings. She encounters unspeakable hardships. She overcomes. She meets Prince Charming. She lives happily ever after.

But what happens when real life hits, and life's circumstances change the story line? You emerge from humble beginnings. You encounter hardship. And more hardship. And more hardship. All the while, voices from those obstacles of the past speak over and over in your head. Hardships keep coming and your Prince Charming doesn't—only those disguised as such. One day you wake up. Your life is half over, and you wonder who you are and what significance you hold to anything or anyone.

My story began in a small college town in southwestern Ohio, where my dad worked at the local post office. We lived in a former schoolhouse built in 1865; a constant, never-finished refurbishing job for my dad. I was the second of eight children, known simply as "one of the Hunter kids" at school and in town. Nothing about me felt distinct from my brothers and sisters—except for my gangly height and long, skinny legs, which only added to my feelings of insecurity.

My parents became Christians when I was six months old, and they helped plant a church almost one hour away in rural Indiana, where Dad eventually pastored. We attended services on Wednesday nights, Saturday nights, Sunday mornings, and to avoid the long drive home, we stayed in the area all day Sunday for the Sunday-evening prayer meetings. We spent almost half of our lives in this way, year after year, in a place where few people even graduated from high school. The rest of the week we lived in a college town, where higher education was the norm.

Spiritually, I just rode along with my parents' faith and depended on their prayers, never making a real commitment of my own. An incident at church one night represented the conflicts I faced. As I knelt at the altar, two people came to pray with me. One stood in front of me saying, "Hold on, Lynda." The other person stood behind me saying, "Just let go, Lynda. Let go."

Hold on? Let go? High school? College? This group? That group? All these emotions collided within me. Then I won a one-year scholarship to the college in our town and worked at three jobs to put myself the rest of the way through school. A little more than three years later, I became the first college graduate in the history of either side of my family when I earned a degree in elementary education. I remember feeling that for the first time, something was just mine. I accepted my first teaching job and began work on my master's degree in education, but my conflict in identity continued. Soon after, I met a non-Christian man, whom I married.

Two years later, I was six-weeks pregnant with our first child. One June Sunday afternoon, I rode above the left tractor wheel while my husband mowed paths for a trail ride we would host the next weekend. After a couple of hours, we ran over a mound of earth hidden by debris in the path. The tractor tipped and threw me into the air. The tire grabbed a pair of jeans tied around my waist and dragged me under the wheel, pinning my left ankle beneath it. I lay on the ground in my own blood, watching the gasoline drip in the front and the bush hog run behind. Then I looked up at the man I had married, the person to whom I'd entrusted my life. He helplessly moved the gears this way and that. Finally the tractor rolled forward enough to allow me to slide out, and I dragged myself to the other side of the path. I lay there wondering how badly I'd been hurt and about the welfare of my baby. I looked way above the tall trees to where I could barely see the blue skies, and suddenly I remembered a verse: "God is our refuge and strength, an ever-present help in trouble" (Psalm 46:1).

A trip to the doctor revealed a broken ankle and a bunch of gashes and bruises that took some time to heal. But something about that incident made me know I had to find my own relationship with God and stop depending on other people for meaning. It would be a while before I would actually make that commitment, however.

Ashley was born in February and Courtney a couple of years later in April. My parents—the ones I still depended on for prayer—moved to Arizona, and Dad got cancer. Then, shortly after learning I was pregnant with our third child, my husband informed me he didn't want to be married anymore. With my dad dying and my husband discarding me, I was losing the last vestige of solidity in my life. At that point, in September 1985, I surrendered my life to Christ. In a field behind our home where the horses grazed, I sat on a rock with a Bible in my lap and prayed, "I give you not just this situation, I give you my whole life."

I heard no voice from heaven, but life changed for me that day. In the weeks and months that followed, I pored over the Bible and talked to Him about the intense pain I felt.

In September 1987, when my children were six, four, and two, we moved some seventy miles away to Ohio, where I enrolled at the University of Cincinnati. We found a church that became home to us, while I worked for the next three years as a teaching assistant and earned my doctorate in the area of curriculum and corporate training. After I finished my degree, I taught at Miami University, worked in my own consulting business, and began to write. In 1994, Focus on the Family asked me to become the editor of their new *Single-Parent Family* magazine, and my family and I moved to Colorado Springs.

Fifteen years have passed since I turned my life over to Christ. The years have been marked by busyness and drivenness. One day I forced myself to look back and reevaluate my life. Though I walked with the Lord, was I still trying to prove something to someone? Still trying to find my significance through accomplishments? Still trying to prove myself as something more than just one of the Hunter kids or a wife who did not deserve leaving?

One morning on the way to work in Colorado, I listened to the report of school and business closures due to snow. "All nonessential personnel need not report today." The term stuck in my mind. Because of the work I'd done with single parents and the experiences I'd been through, I knew what it felt like to be nonessential personnel. A nonessential wife. A nonessential mother. A nonessential single woman. I thought about those who hear the words: "We've eliminated your position." "I've found a younger woman." "We won't be needing your services anymore." Nonessential—often the story of our lives.

Individual Scripts

The stories of our lives consist of what has happened to us to make us feel as we do, how we respond, and where we're going from here. Shakespeare once wrote, "All the world's a stage, and all the men and women merely players." Psychologists tell us that the way each of us feels about ourselves is the product of various events within our own life stories. These narratives contain a larger purpose; a beginning, middle, and end; and they share common elements, such as characters, plot, key events, turning points, and themes.

When I taught junior high English, I decorated a bulletin board with the different types, or genres, of stories: those with happy endings or sad. Happy-ending stories include comedy (characters overcome obstacles to find happiness) and romance (characters strike out on a quest or journey). Sad-ending stories include tragedy (characters are overcome by inescapable changes or absurdities) and irony (characters are caught up in the mysteries, ambiguities, and contradictions of life).

Though a Christian's story will ultimately be a happy one, sometimes the earlier chapters stink. We mask feelings of low self-esteem with pretty dresses and trite talk and filled schedules. All the while, we fail to pinpoint or even acknowledge the anger and pain we feel. Then when things don't go as we expect them to, or we encounter rejection, we blame people or circumstances or decide it doesn't matter anyway. Discontent follows, and we begin our search to fill the empty places. We seek success and love and acclaim from others, hoping that through all our hard work, we will at last find significance.

Someone's wife, someone's mother, someone's child, someone's employee. But who are we with the possessives aside, all else stripped away, and we stand naked in front of the mirror?

"Who Am I?" It's Not a New Question

Significance is not defined in the Bible, but God's Word is filled with people whose faith impacted the way they felt about themselves. Even Moses, David, and Solomon asked "Who am I?"

Moses. Moses was born to parents from the priestly tribe of Israel, during a time when the pharaoh had ordered that all Jewish boy babies be destroyed. So Jochebed, Moses' mother, placed him in a basket and released him to the bulrush. His sister watched from afar as the daughter of the pharaoh found him, and Moses was raised as her own in Pharaoh's palace. One day, after he was grown, Moses saw an Egyptian strike a Jew, and he killed the Egyptian and hid his body in the sand. Moses fled for his life and stayed in Midian some forty years. Then God heard the repeated cries of His people for relief from persecution. He appeared to Moses one day in a burning bush, and told him he'd been chosen to free the Israelites. Moses questioned his significance and qualifications for the job eleven times, beginning with "*Who am I?* that I should go to Pharaoh and bring the Israelites out of Egypt?" (Exodus 3:11, emphasis added).

David. David was anointed king by Samuel, then he went on to kill Goliath. His fame spread, and so did the jealousy of King Saul, who tried many times to kill him. David ran, and 1 Samuel 18:14 tells us, he "behaved himself wisely in all his ways; and the LORD was with him" (KJV). Eventually Saul died and David became king. "Then King David went in and sat before the LORD, and he said: '*Who am I,* O Sovereign LORD, and what is my family, that you have brought me this far?'" (2 Samuel 7:18, emphasis added).

After his triumphs as well as his defeats, his good moves as well as his bad, David prayed just before he died: "Now, our God, we give you thanks, and praise your glorious name. But *who am I,* and who are my people, that we should be able to give as generously as this? Everything comes from you, and we have given you only what comes from your hand" (1 Chronicles 29:13–14, emphasis added).

Solomon. David's son, Solomon, became king after his father's death. Solomon prepared to build the temple when he prayed, "But who is able to build a temple for him, since the heavens, even the highest heavens, cannot contain him? *Who then am I* to build a temple for him, except as a place to burn sacrifices before him?" (2 Chronicles 2:6, emphasis added).

Three men of ancient times asked the same question you and I ask today: "Who am I?" Eventually they realized that they were nothing without God, but everything through Him. They relinquished the identities they never had as human beings to embrace the identities they had always had through God. Also like you and me, these men exhibited weaknesses: Moses murdered the Egyptian, David committed adultery, and Solomon worshiped other gods. They asked the question, but they asked it of God. And their lives reflected the journey each took toward finding their significance through Him.

We also find many women emerge as examples of Godly significance, though they lived in a time when women were looked down upon and regarded as insignificant. Two of these women, Rahab and Ruth, even became ancestors in the lineage of Christ. Rahab, though a pillar of Bible history, was not a pillar of the community. As a harlot, she moved beyond her sullied past and helped Joshua and his men hide out in Jericho in exchange for the safety of her family (Joshua 2:1–21). She later married an Israelite named Salmon and gave birth to a child named Boaz.

A woman named Ruth watched her husband, father-in-law, and brother-in-law die. She looked beyond her inferior bloodline as a Moabite and followed her mother-in-law and the god she served back to Bethlehem. There she married Rahab's son, Boaz, and Ruth became the great-grandmother, and Rahab the great-great-grandmother, of King David, and ancestors of Jesus Christ. Whether their gender, their past, or their bloodlines, Rahab and Ruth made their questions of insignificance become obstacles to insignificance, as they presented themselves before God to become all they had been designed to be.

Your Story's Story

It's time for you to do the same. For whatever reason, your story may be comedy or romance, tragedy or irony—or any combination of them all. No matter what the content of your chapters thus far, you can be assured that a happy ending awaits all of us who trust in God. Your story and mine are smaller stories within a larger one where God plays center stage and has everything—the setting, conflicts, characters, themes, and resolutions—under complete control. Realizing this and moving that realization from head knowledge to heart knowledge makes our story more enjoyable along the way.

The material in this book can't do anything about what has happened to you in previous life chapters, but it can help you write future ones. I have identified ten areas as the most problematic for women I've worked with in their quests for significance. When you finish reading the book, you will be able to say with conviction:

1. I am making a choice
2. I am armed
3. I am loved
4. I am free
5. I am growing
6. I am forgiven and forgiving
7. I am finding intimacy
8. I am called
9. I am passing it on
10. I am significant

In addition, you will realize your own story's:

1. story
2. revision process
3. bigger story
4. conflicts
5. character growth

6. plots
7. theme
8. purpose
9. relationship to others' stories
10. resolution

Like Moses, David, Solomon, Rahab, and Ruth, we can find our significance through God by asking the right question of the right source. If we're in Christ, we already know how the book ends. But we can also enjoy the chapters in between. We read in John 10:10 (NASB), "The thief comes only to steal, and kill, and destroy; I came that they might have life, and might have it abundantly."

Not just eternal life, but abundant life too. That includes living a life of significance, making the most of what life offers, and revising undesirable chapters. May God guide you as you find answers to your own question, "Who am I . . . really?"

CHAPTER 1

I Am Making a Choice

Realizing Your Story

"I have been crucified with Christ and I no longer live, but Christ lives in me. The life I live in the body, I live by faith in the Son of God, who loved me and gave himself for me."

—GALATIANS 2:20

My oldest daughter, Ashley, had just turned sixteen months old when I embarked upon the potty-training process with her. One day as she sat in the bathroom swinging her crossed ankles, she said, "Me, my, Ashley. They're all the same." And she raised her arms in celebration of her new discovery.

Ashley realized even at a young age that her life had a story to tell. It had its own time and place, and it featured, "Me, my, Ashley" as the central character. But examining this concept of self has not always been as much an option as it is today. The Oxford English Dictionary gives 1674 as the first citation for the usage of self as the individual person. Before that time a separate word didn't exist, and people associated themselves only with the group—family, tribe, or village—to which they belonged.

Some time between the Renaissance and the Industrial Revolution, however, Western society became more complex and differentiated. One person no longer seemed the same as everyone else. Literature, philosophy, and social thought started focusing on the individual. In literature, novels began to record stories about individual people. In philosophy, Descartes and Locke examined the world from the individual's point of view. In political thought, Hobbes, Locke, and Rousseau contrasted the individual with the state.

Within this setting, the word and idea of self as we now know it developed in personality psychology. To society, self became a way to preserve a sense of continuity in the midst of change, identity in the midst of diversity, and the quest to find individual significance within our own worlds. People started asking, "Who am I?" and, "Who am I to be?" as they tried to find their identities, their sense of place in the world, and their meaning in life.

Today, in the midst of the many choices and opportunities women find, never have more of us wondered where we fit in and what value we hold. The phrase "feel good about yourself" has become a cliché in pop psychology. Personal-development magazines at the supermarket lines are filled with the latest tips and techniques for raising one's self-esteem and sense of worth. My friend Bonnie Shepherd once said to an elderly woman she knew, "I don't know how you made it during a time when you didn't have many choices."

The woman responded, "I don't know how you make it now that you do."

Unfortunately, choices we have; high self-esteem we often don't. Christians fare no better in this area than those who don't know Christ. Though a personal relationship with Jesus can give us access to all we're created to be, and we can become eternally significant through Him, we miss the target because we aim at the wrong places and believe the wrong things. Some of us observe our unfulfilled dreams and wonder where we missed the boat. Others of us watch our boat sail out of sight as we support the dreams of someone else, such as a husband or a child. And we can't seem to please a society that implies a single woman needs to have a husband and children, but a married woman can't find fulfillment by being "just" a wife and mother. There's always someone smarter or prettier or richer or more capable or more important. These factors all place us on the side of a battle we can never win.

SELF-SIGNIFICANCE

Simply stated, significance is defined as "the importance or value assigned to a person or thing." Self-significance explains what we believe about ourselves. It has no concrete existence in itself as defined by our five senses. Even if our importance is recognized by others in specific settings, significance will not be felt unless we recognize this importance ourselves. A positive feeling of self-significance means you have a sense of being someone of value to yourself and to others, and you hold a realistic view of your strengths and weaknesses. A negative sense of self-significance can result in you feeling:

- invaluable
- incapable
- hesitant to try new things
- fearful
- pessimistic in your view of work and your ability to cope with challenges
- intimidated and threatened by the unexpected or new
- pushed and crushed by the rest of the world
- victimized and trapped in a hostile environment
- lacking confidence
- oversensitive to others' opinions

- self-conscience about your appearance, performance, and status
- in competition with others
- pressured to be somebody instead of enjoying who you are
- driven to use sexual prowess

Because each of us arrives at our own constantly changing mental image of ourselves as the result of certain episodes in our life stories, good experiences—such as a healthy family or economic privilege—can impact our opinions positively. On the other hand, bad experiences—such as poverty or divorce—can negatively affect our opinions of ourselves and others. As a result, we can spend a lifetime searching for love, acceptance, and success, without seeing the need for God that compels us. Apart from Him, we believe lies that look something like this:

- I can't win against the bad stuff.
- No one really loves me.
- I can't get over my past.
- I've got too many faults.
- I can't forgive.
- I don't know how to get close to others.
- I'm not talented.
- My life won't make a difference.
- I'm not significant.

To compound the problem even more, we hear from the pulpit two lines of thinking: one follows the crowd in a quest for self-esteem, the other touts as sin even asking questions about our self-worth. So what's a Christian to do? Remain in limbo? Go with the world's search? Deny the questions we feel? Is our quest for significance and knowing ourselves permitting anti-Christian values to enter our Christian lives? Are we exchanging holiness, obedience, and personal sacrifice for affirmation? Is the idea of self-image only another effort to focus selfish attention on ourselves?

God-significance

I believe a healthy self-image—deepening one's own dignity and purpose—is a blessing offered to those who know Christ. I believe it's God's good pleasure to supply a feeling of significance to those who belong to Him. Since what society calls poor self-image is really a poor God-image, the place to build the former is to work on the latter. You hand over your questions of self-worth to God as you deepen your walk with Him, and He hands them back whole and significant. It's what I call God-significance.

Self-significance enthrones the work of the individual, de-emphasizes the need for salvation, and doesn't allow for human error. God-significance, on the other hand, can never be earned, and it elevates the work of God through man's strengths as well as his weaknesses. God-significance allows you to see the world as a challenge to be faced and an opportunity to exercise personal strength and trust in God. He designed the emptiness and the searching inside each of us to drive us to Himself. God-significance comes through grace to all people who will receive it.

God is the author of individuality, after all. God-significance offers strength and humility, sorrow over sin as well as joy about forgiveness, and the knowledge that we are nothing without Christ and everything through Him. In *My Utmost for His Highest* (Thomas

Nelson, 1993), Oswald Chambers writes: "The bedrock in Jesus Christ's kingdom is poverty, not possessions; not decision for Jesus Christ, but a sense of absolute futility. 'I cannot do it alone.' Then Jesus says, 'Blessed are you.' I cannot enter His kingdom as a good man or woman, I can only enter it as a complete pauper."

The Bible tells us in Romans 12:3: "For by the grace given me I say to every one of you: Do not to think of yourself more highly than you ought, but rather think of yourself with sober judgment, in accordance with the measure of faith God has given you."

So how do we achieve significance without catering to self?

SCRIPTURE

"DO NOT THINK OF YOURSELF MORE HIGHLY THAN YOU OUGHT . . ."

Sometimes in our search for significance, we elevate our importance and place it above that of others. The disciples, for example, had heard Jesus preach the Sermon on the Mount and the Beatitudes, and give instructions on how to pray. They had seen Him still the storm, walk on water, stretch two fishes and five loaves of bread to feed five thousand, and heal the blind, mute, palsied, and leprous people. Certainly the disciples saw themselves as privileged, perhaps too much so, as evidenced by the question they asked in Matthew 18:1: "Who is the greatest in the kingdom of heaven?"

Jesus brought a child close and answered their question with these simple words: "Whoever humbles himself like this child is the greatest in the kingdom of heaven" (Matthew 18:4).

And then there was Zebedee's wife, the mother of disciples James and John. Like any mother, she wanted the best life had to offer for her boys. She bowed before Jesus and asked that her sons become candidates for thrones No. 2 and No. 3 behind Jesus: "Grant that one of these two sons of mine may sit at your right and the other at your left in your kingdom" (Matthew 20:21).

But Jesus called them to Himself and said, " . . . whoever wants to become great among you must be your servant, and whoever wants to be first must be your slave—just as the Son of Man did not come to be served, but to serve, and to give his life as a ransom for many" (Matthew 20:26–28).

What? Some help Jesus was. Their questions had to do with their significance, yet He told them to become like children and servants? Doesn't make sense. Or does it?

The word servant is defined as "a person who serves the needs or purposes of another often out of devotion." Jesus showed by His example. He pushed up His sleeves and washed the disciples' feet, then said, "I have set you an example that you should do as I have done for you. . . . Now that you know these things, you will be blessed if you do them" (John 13:15, 17).

I had signed for the big bucks at my first teaching job—$7,300 per year. After only a few weeks, I began to wonder, *Is this all there is? Is this the place I worked so hard to reach?*

One day I decided to look outside myself, and I walked three doors up from my apartment to a nursing home. After obtaining permission, I bought craft supplies and went every Thursday night to work with the ladies at the home. We'd do crafts, sing, and pray together. Every week I'd walk there grudgingly, then I would float home. Somewhere in between, I forgot the mundane questions I'd asked earlier and saw life in the bigger picture, rather than looking through a drinking straw. I got a little taste of what it meant to be a servant by offering some of my gifts to others. And that's God's design. We read in 1 Peter 4:10: "Each one should use whatever gift he has received to serve others, faithfully administering God's grace in its various forms."

At the church my dad pastored, we held what we called "camp meeting" on the third Sunday in August. After the noon service, each family brought their specialty dishes to the side yard and displayed them on tables made of boards supported by sawhorses. Lucy baked her butterscotch brownies. Nellie brought chicken and dumplings. My mom offered different kinds of homemade pies. The result? We all ate like kings and queens. So whose dish was the most important to the meal?

The apostle Paul wrote a manuscript in Macedonia and needed someone to deliver it for him to Rome. He called on Phoebe, a single woman, and asked her to carry his message (Romans 16:1–2). Phoebe cleared her schedule, took Paul's writings to Rome, and acted as his spokesperson for three years until Paul could arrive himself. These writings became the book of Romans—the most complete declaration of the gospel to the Gentiles—and from there spread to the rest of the world. So who was the greatest: Paul who wrote Romans or Phoebe who delivered it?

I have a friend named Susan who witnessed for twelve years to another friend of hers, Nancy, who was an atheist. Nancy seemed to pay no heed to those years of Susan telling her about God. One day, Susan called me with excitement in her voice. "Guess what? A perfect stranger just led Nancy to the Lord. Can you believe it?" So who was the greatest: Susan who faithfully witnessed for twelve years, or the woman who shared her faith with Nancy that day?

Another friend of mine, Jerry, walked into a church one morning where he didn't know anyone. Jerry still reeled from a divorce that had left him rejected, depressed, and alone. All the possessions that remained after twenty-six years of marriage were stuffed into the back of his car. That morning a man named Rudy, who directed cars in the parking lot, shook Jerry's hand, looked him in the eyes, and deposited love into the depths of his aching soul. For several Sundays that followed, this interaction continued outside the church doors. Not long after that, someone led Jerry to the Lord. So who was the greatest: Rudy, who showed love week after week to the man who felt unlovely, or the person who actually prayed with Jerry the sinner's prayer?

Who's the greatest? People have diverse talents, gifts, and abilities. Paul told us to work for unity in the midst of diversity and not to compare (2 Corinthians 10:12). Jesus told us to be servants and to give the gifts that we have. We each hold a piece to the puzzle, but the picture belongs to Him. We've all labored over puzzles only to get to the end and find a piece or two missing. To withhold the gifts we possess creates a similar hole in God's big picture.

I know a woman whose husband insisted she get an abortion. "We aren't ready for a family yet," he said. After the procedure ended, the woman went to her doctor's office for a follow-up visit. She stole the documents from her files, carried them from the office, and shredded them, hoping to also shred the memory that she had destroyed a life. But now more than a decade later, she still wonders who her child might have become. What if someone truly "great" or "significant" had been there for that woman in crisis—a friend to cry with or a person marching at the clinic making women like her aware of the years of consequences to follow?

God gifts His children, then He asks us to give those gifts back to His work, wherever they are needed. That makes each piece significant, because it's part of the whole.

When my children were young, I read to them from a book called *Together* (Orchard Books, 1989) by George Ella Lyon. Part of it went like this:

I'll drive the truck, if you'll fight the fire
I'll plunk the keys, if you'll be the choir
I'll find the ball, if you'll call the team
Let's put our heads together and dream the same dream.

You dig for water, and I'll make a pail
I'll paint the boat, if you'll set the sail
You catch the fish, and I'll catch the stream
Let's put our heads together and dream the same dream.

Having a servant's heart means understanding God's dream, then dreaming it with Him. It means me humbly offering what I have combined with you offering what you have, and together making God's big picture. And those who do? They are the greatest—the most significant—in the kingdom of God.

". . . Think of Yourself with Sober Judgment"

We can think too highly of ourselves, as did the disciples and the mother of James and John. Other times we underestimate our value before God. Because of previous chapters in our life stories, we may deem ourselves unworthy to be used by God. Though Jesus told us to be servants, we should be careful not to confuse servanthood with disqualification. There are those who carry such low opinions of themselves that they never dare talk to God. Why would He bother to listen to someone as menial as they are, after all? As a result, they miss out on the blessings God has for them.

Bob's wife left him and their two children as their oldest child headed off to kindergarten. Life overwhelmed him, and he felt intense rejection. On top of everything else he had to do, a limb had broken loose from a tree in front of his house. It had to be cut down carefully or it would fall on the house. Bob would either have to take time off from work to cut down the limb himself or hire someone else to do it. He couldn't afford either. So he prayed. That night, a storm blew in. Bob awoke to find the limb lying neatly on the ground in front of his house.

Jesus encountered people like Bob who had reached the bottom, had low self-esteems, and felt unworthy to bring their problems before Him. But they did. Jesus found that surrender pleasing, and He answered their requests.

In Matthew 8, we read the story of how Jesus journeyed to Capernaum, and a centurion—the commander of one hundred soldiers in the Roman army—came to him asking for help. "'Lord,' he said, 'my servant lies at home paralyzed and in terrible suffering'" (Matthew 8:6).

Jesus offered to go and heal him, but the centurion replied, "Lord, I do not deserve to have you come under my roof. But just say the word, and my servant will be healed" (v. 8). He went on to explain his unworthiness and his belief in Jesus' power to command that something be done.

Jesus disregarded the man's explanations of his unworthiness and honored his faith as He said, "Go! It will be done just as you believed it would" (v. 13). And the servant was healed that very hour.

We read of another incident in Matthew 15:21–28 when Jesus acknowledged the faith of a woman who persisted in her request to Him, despite her feelings of insignificance. Jesus had gone to Tyre and Sidon for some quiet time. A Canaanite woman came to him and said, "Lord, Son of David, have mercy on me! My daughter is suffering terribly from demon-possession" (v. 22).

Jesus didn't answer, and the disciples urged Him to send the woman away. But she persisted with her request. Jesus, challenging her own feelings of significance, told the woman that He'd been sent to the Jews. She knelt before him and begged for help, but Jesus continued to speak about His chosen people, "It is not right to take the children's bread and toss it to their dogs" (v. 26).

The woman knew that she was unimportant as a Canaanite. But her feelings of insignificance were overshadowed by her humility and persistence in seeking help for her daughter. This moved Jesus, and He answered, "Woman, you have great faith! Your request is granted" (v. 28). And, like the centurion's servant, her daughter was healed that very hour.

Application

The disciples and James and John's mother learned that they could never be good enough to earn significance in Christ. The centurion and the woman with the sick daughter discovered that they could never be too low, too unimportant, to matter to Him. All of them learned the difference between self-significance and God-significance, and that pride and self-denigration are two sides of the same coin, both of which interfere with God's plan for His people. The greatness that Jesus talked about cannot be found in self-exaltation but in humility. God-significance does not come by concern for self but through concern for others. It's only as we give our efforts that we receive God's praise. It's only as we surrender our self-significance that we gain God-significance. To be great, we become nothing. To raise self-esteem, we die to self. We let go of all to gain all.

The disciples, the centurion, the woman, and you and I. We matter because we matter to God. We're significant because we're significant to God—so much so that He sent His Son for us: "For you know that it was not with perishable things such as silver or gold that you were redeemed from the empty way of life handed down to you from your forefathers, but with the precious blood of Christ, a lamb without blemish or defect. He was chosen before the creation of the world, but was revealed in these last times for your sake" (1 Peter 1:18–20).

We read in Galatians 2:20 how Paul put on the new self of God-significance: "I have been crucified with Christ and I no longer live, but Christ lives in me." He broke free of self-realization and became crucified with Christ. He signed away his own rights and became a bond slave of Jesus Christ. When we do the same, the previous list of self-significant lies changes to look like this:

SELF-SIGNIFICANCE		GOD-SIGNIFICANCE
I live on my own →	I am crucified (Surrender) →	Christ lives in me

LIES	TRUTH
I can't win against the bad stuff.	I am armed.
No one really loves me.	I am loved.
I can't get over my past.	I am free.
I've got too many faults.	I am growing.
I can't forgive.	I am forgiven and forgiving.
I don't know how to get close to others.	I am finding intimacy.
I'm not talented.	I am called.
My life won't make a difference.	I am passing it on.
I'm not significant.	I am significant.

James and John, as well as the centurion and the unnamed woman, recognized Jesus as the Son of God. They came to Him as imperfect but committed vessels. You and I need to do the same—come to Christ. The best time to receive Him was years ago; the second best time is right now. He longs to restore some of the things that have been stolen from you. If you already know Christ, be sure you do not have unconfessed sin in your life. Once the issue of salvation is settled, know that victory is assured for those who trust in Him as their personal Savior. Then pursue a life of realizing your significance from this day on by:

Knowing the truth, rejecting the lie. Satan attacks your vulnerable areas. The way you view yourself becomes the lens through which you see what's real and what's not, the truth vs. the lie. Based on how you see things, you choose your behavior according to the situation. If your lens distorts the situation, you won't deal properly with reality. The better you feel about yourself, the more you see the truth, reject the lie, and react accordingly.

Let's go back to the centurion and the woman with the demon-possessed daughter. The lie prevented them from believing they mattered to Christ. But when Jesus dispelled that myth, they believed and received His blessing that had been there waiting for them to accept all along. You can do the same by knowing and living so closely to the truth of God's Word that it dispels the lies you face every day.

Concentrating on servanthood. Servanthood has its roots in a healthy self-image. It means you've turned loose of everything to follow God.

One day I had lunch with my friend Susie Shellenberger, editor of *Brio* magazine. She talked about an injustice she had suffered and what she planned to do about it. But when we met for lunch a week or so later, she sang a different tune. Susie told me she had gone for a speaking engagement after our talk, still livid about her treatment. Then God spoke to her heart with these words: *You can hold on to your rights, but when you became Mine, you gave them up. Let Me fight your battles for you.*

Susie found an answer for her problem and peace for her heart at the same time, because she chose the high road to servanthood. When I see women grasp this concept instead of asking, "What about me?" their marriages and other relationships strengthen. They become more content and peaceful, knowing that God holds their best interests close to His heart.

Surrendering your life to God. I heard a story once of a woman who heard God say to her, "I want everything you have."

"Everything?" the woman said. "Even the $7,000 my husband and I have saved?"

"Everything. I even want your boat."

"I suppose you want my RV too."

"Oh, you have an RV?"

"Here's my car and house. And what about my husband and children? You'll want them too."

"Okay, then. Now that I have everything, I'm going to give them back to you to use for a while. But always remember from whose hand you received them."

Ladies, it all belongs to Him. The gifts and power to use them are given to us so we can serve others, so that we can give them away. We are not to realize ourselves, but to truly know God in us. We aren't to just come to Christ, but to surrender everything to Him as well. We have to give up our own significance to receive the eternal significance offered through Christ.

God's purpose is not to develop men and women with high self-esteems, but to make us like Himself through His Son, the very representation of self-expenditure and servanthood. It's not what we gain from knowing Christ, but what He pours through us that counts. God gave His Son so sinners could be saved. We should pour out our lives too, and significance will follow.

Conclusion

When I was a child, my dad left his work car outside the garage at night. In winter he would place a piece of cardboard on the windshield so he wouldn't have to scrape ice or snow on those early Ohio mornings. Before Dad headed to work, however, he had to take the cardboard off the windshield and put it into the trunk, because he couldn't see above or below, around or through it. It remained an obstruction to going forward until he took it away.

Our difficulties and questions in life can loom in front of us, in much the same way as the cardboard would have, had it not been removed. God tells us to present our problems to Him every day and to ignore the important questions of significance. He wants us to bring them before Him daily, read His Word for direction, counsel with godly people, then go forward doing the work He's called us to that day. God doesn't want us to allow these questions to become so big in front of us that they prevent us from moving forward or being the servant He's called us to be. After all, He needs the piece of the puzzle you hold in your hand. Don't waste it hiding behind the cardboard.

Bible Study

As you can see, the Bible's version of self-esteem is not the same as the world's. The Bible tells us that spiritual things can't be understood by the world (1 Corinthians 2:14). But because you and I know Christ, we can know the truth through Him.

Paradox is a statement that appears to contradict itself or be contrary to common sense. G. K. Chesterton says, "Paradox is truth standing on its head to get attention." Examine these apparent paradoxes in Scripture:

Regarding wealth. The world says: Get all you can get.

God says: To get wealth, __________. (Proverbs 13:7; 2 Corinthians 6:4, 8–10)

Regarding intelligence. The world says: Get smart.

God says: To get intelligence, ______________. (1 Corinthians 3:18; Ephesians 3:17–19)

Regarding strength. The world says: Get rid of your weaknesses.

God says: To be strong, get ________. (2 Corinthians 12:9).

Regarding getting ahead. The world says: Go for it.

God says, To get ahead, __________ (Philippians 3:7).

Regarding self-esteem. The world says: Find yourself.

God says: To find yourself, __________ (Matthew 10:39, 16:25; Mark 8:35; Luke 17:33; John 12:25).

Not self-significance . . .

Sin is claiming my right to myself. Be careful of pride, which leads to self-worship and to usurping God's control. It points back to self instead of the true source.

PHILIPPIANS 2:3–5: "Do nothing out of ___________ _________ or ________ ___________, but in humility consider others ___________ than _________________. Each of you should look not only to your own ___________________, but also to the _______________ of ______________. Your attitude should be the same as that of Christ Jesus."

PHILIPPIANS 3:9: "Not having a righteousness of my own that comes from the ______, but that which is through

__________ in ______________ ____________—the righteousness that comes from God and is by _____________."

1 CORINTHIANS 8:2–3: "The man who thinks he _______ ________ does not yet know as he ought to know. But the man who ________ _____ is __________ by God."

. . . but God-significance.

Gain your God-significance by relinquishing your self-significance.

LEVITICUS 19:18; MATTHEW 19:19; MARK 12:31; LUKE 10:27; ROMANS 13:9: "Love your _________ as _____________." This verse is listed by Jesus as the second greatest commandment.

COLOSSIANS 3:1–5, 7–10: "Since, then, you have been raised with Christ, set your _________ on things above, where Christ is seated at the right hand of God. Set your _________ on things above, not on earthly things. For you died, and your life is now _______ with ________ in God. When Christ, who is your life, appears, then you also will appear with him in glory. Put to death, therefore, whatever belongs to your _______ _______. . . . You used to walk in these ways, in the life you once lived. But now you must _____ _________ of all such things as these. . . . since you have taken off your ______ ________ with its practices and have put on the _______ ________, which is being ____________ in ___________ in the image of its Creator."

And what about servanthood?

We read in Romans 1:1 (NASB): "Paul, a bond-servant of _______ ______, called as an _________, set apart for the _______ ___ ______."

"A bond-servant of Jesus Christ." A servant serves his master out of duty and is often bound by law. A bond-servant serves voluntarily until his death, out of love and respect for his master. To mark him as a bond-servant, the master pierces the servant's ear "with an awl. Then he will be his servant for life" (Exodus 21:6). The noted expository teacher Donald Grey Barnhouse compares the servant with the bond-servant: "Any man in the army knows the difference between the soldier who kicked against the whole system and the soldier who yielded himself fully to his duty." So when Paul called himself a bond-servant, he meant that he was giving himself wholeheartedly to God.

In his book *The MacArthur Topical Bible* (Word Publishing, 1999), John MacArthur tells us that honor through subservience comes only through grace: "There is, of course, an honor and dignity attached to all of God's true servants, even the most seemingly insignificant, and Paul was very much aware of the undeserved but real dignity God bestows on those who belong to Him. He was constantly aware also that the dignity and honor God gives His children are purely from grace, that in themselves, Christians are still sinful, depraved and undeserving. . . . the emphasis is on subservience and insignificance, not honor."

What does becoming a bond-servant mean to your life's significance? ____

"Called as an apostle." Paul did not make his own assignment into ministry: God called him. "[He] is my chosen instrument to carry my name before the Gentiles and their kings and before the people of Israel" (Acts 9:15). The term apostle means, "One sent with a special message or commission," and can be used to refer to all believers, who are called to tell the world about Christ.

What does being called mean to your life's significance?

____

"Set apart for the gospel of God." Paul knew that being called by God to witness to the world sets one apart. Separated unto God. You can't be effective unless you're set apart (Leviticus 20:26; Exodus 13:12; Numbers 15:11–14, 20). In the Septuagint, the word translated "present," "lift up," and "set apart" is the same: *aphorizo,* i.e., the firstborn, an offering, the priestly tribe. This allows no mixing of the chosen Jews with Gentile nations in marriage, or of the sacred with the profane and ordinary. Paul was set apart divinely from his mother's womb (Galatians 1:15).

What does being set apart mean to your life's significance?

____

Dear God:

You know everything about me (Psalm 139), so you know I struggle in the area of self-worth. I now understand through Your Word that the way to gain my worth is to be crucified with You and to allow You to live through me. The way to be great is to become like a servant and a child. The way to overcome my feelings of low self-esteem is to present these feelings to You and then grow as a Christian. The way to refute the lies is to recognize the truth. And the way to gain self-significance is to claim my God-significance (Galatians 2:20). Help me as I begin the journey to find my reason for being, by finding my significance in You. In the name of Jesus Christ, amen.

CHAPTER 2

I Am Armed

Revising Your Story

"In all these things we
are more than conquerors
through him who
loved us."

—ROMANS 8:37

I sat across the table from thirty-one-year-old Tina. Married to a successful doctor, she stayed at home to raise four beautiful children ranging in ages from two to eight. Tina seemed to have it all. The chips and salsa remained untouched, however, as she spoke from her heart. She expressed love for her husband and children, but she described feelings of monotony and a lack of purpose. She'd grown up in the church and knew the right scriptures—even sang in the choir. But my heart ached for Tina as she described her pain: "If only I had work that I could pour myself into to give meaning to my life."

I couldn't help but remember talking recently to Amy, a single woman around the same age as Tina, and also a Christian. She spoke about the job she loved, but she described her lack of direction and fulfillment. "I just want to get married and have children. I feel so unimportant. That's all I want. Is that wrong?"

The feeling of insignificance knows no gender, socioeconomic, or marital barriers. Amy thinks that finding the right man will fill the empty places in her life. Tina has discovered that the right man doesn't, and she continues her search for significance in other places. Each wants what the other has already found unfulfilling.

Like Tina and Amy, when we find that we've lost our enthusiasm, our devotion to a cause, or our energetic and unflagging pursuit of a goal, we start to look for a way out. We blame our circumstances for our lack of zeal. We seek other paths for our lives to take. Or worse yet, we head in the direction of recapturing a dream, only to decide it's too difficult to attain, and we run back to the familiar, the mundane, the mediocre—where we sometimes live out the rest of our lives. Author Evan S. Connell writes, "Some people go skimming over the years of existence to sink gently into a placid grave, ignorant of life to the last, without ever having been made to see all it may contain" *(Mrs. Bridge,* Viking Press, 1959).

To understand these struggles, we need to look at our history as human beings. All good stories provide background information, and if we don't know the details of the past, we're powerless to deal with the present or the future. Too many of us think we're destined for spiritual warfare on earth (which we are) and doomed to defeat (which we aren't). We need to find out what happened in the beginning to make things as they are today, and what we can do to revise our story—make new, amend, improve—and create an up-to-date version. Our faith in Christ equips us to do that.

Just as our life stories have a beginning, middle, and end, so does the story of life itself. "In the beginning God created the heavens and the earth" (Genesis 1:1). In the end we read, "Behold, I am coming soon! My reward is with me, and I will give to everyone according to what he has done" (Revelation 22:12).

But like Tina and Amy, we're stuck somewhere in the middle, and we often forget the rest of the story. Life gets difficult, and it's hard to imagine things getting any better. To understand the origin of our search for significance, we need to go back to the beginning.

Scripture

In the Beginning . . .

At creation, God equipped man with the essentials for discovering our true significance. We read in Genesis 2 how man's purpose was to honor God and his value came as the special creation of God. And "the LORD God formed man of the dust of the ground, and breathed into his nostrils the breath of life; and man became a living soul" (Genesis 2:7 KJV).

This living soul became one with God as he submitted to His will. Man took his place in the garden God had provided for him, and he got to work caring for the garden and naming the livestock, birds, and beasts. Man also stayed away from the one thing—the tree of the knowledge of good and evil—that God had forbidden.

Then God took a rib from the man and made a helper for him. God called this helper woman. "The man and his wife were both naked, and they felt no shame" (Genesis 2:25), because they were one with God in body, soul, and spirit. And the woman's role looked like this:

- Made in God's image
- Ruled over earthly creatures (Genesis 1:26–28)
- Completed man (Genesis 2:18–25)
- Gave life (Genesis 3:20)

Together the man and woman communed with God. Then the woman listened to the crafty serpent, which urged her to eat of the forbidden tree so she could "be like God" (Genesis 3:5). So she did, the man did, and warfare began. Their bodies became world conscious and began dying a slow death. Their souls turned to self-service and ego gratification, "and they realized they were naked" (Genesis 3:7). Their spirits lost unity and fellowship with God, and they desired to rule above Him. And the woman's role changed to this:

Pre-Fall → Obeyed God	Fall Disobeyed God
Ruled over earthly creatures (Genesis 1:26–28)	Desired to be god-like (Genesis 3:1–7)
Completed man (Genesis 2:18–25)	Desired to rule over man (Genesis 4:7)
Gave life (Genesis 3:20; 4:1)	Increased pain in childbirth (Genesis 3:16)

The conflict continued with all men and women born after them, a battle between soul and spirit, right and wrong, good and bad. The knowledge of God became confused. Those who knew God could barely understand the truths of the spirit. Those who didn't know God couldn't understand these truths at all, as they were only spiritually discerned.

Then God offered a way to take on a new spirit, through the gift of His Son. But change didn't come without resistance.

. . . AND THE END

A pregnant woman appeared in the heavens, clothed with the sun, the moon under her feet. She wore a crown of twelve stars on her head, and she cried out in the pain of childbirth.

Suddenly the crafty serpent appeared on the scene again, wearing ten horns and seven heads. His giant tail swept a third of the stars from the sky and flung them to earth. He stood in front of the woman who was about to give birth to a son. He knew that child would rule all the nations with an iron scepter. "I have to stop him," the serpent said.

So he moved toward the woman, but he was too late. The woman gave birth to a son, who was snatched up to God and His throne. She fled into the desert to a place God had prepared for her. She stayed there many days, and a war broke out. The archangel Michael and his angels fought against the serpent, who had joined forces with his evil companions. But the serpent's forces could not overcome the angels, so the serpent and his angels lost their place in heaven and were hurled to Earth.

That great serpent, called the devil or Satan, set out to lead the whole world astray. But a voice spoke from heaven:

> For the accuser of our brothers,
> who accuses them before our God day and night,
> has been hurled down.
> They overcame him by the blood of the Lamb
> and by the word of their testimony;
> they did not love their lives so much
> as to shrink from death.
> Therefore rejoice, you heavens
> and you who dwell in them!

> But woe to the earth and the sea,
> because the devil has gone down to you!
> He is filled with fury,
> because he knows that his time is short.
> (Revelation 12:10–12)

The serpent hated these words, and he pursued the woman again. But once again, God helped her escape the serpent's grasp.

This infuriated the serpent. He spit water like a river and tried once more to overtake the woman. But the earth became her friend and swallowed the river.

Unable to reach the woman or her child, the enraged serpent went off to make war against the rest of her offspring—those who obey God's commandments and hold to the testimony of Jesus—because he knew his time was short.

And now, nearly two thousand years after John received these visions, Satan still wars against those who obey God's commandments. Among those he attacks are women in all walks of life who struggle with meaning in their lives. Satan pounces with both feet. He roars and spits. He makes noises and works hard to persuade them that they've lost the battle. In the Fall, men and women exchanged their secure status with God for pride, inadequacy, desperation, and a regard for men's opinions more than God's. Though creation tended toward life, health, and growth, the curse leads to death, decay, and suffering. Now everything is wearing out, running down, getting old, and succumbing to more and more disorder.

The Fall took real self and replaced it with a life-long search for significance through what we do and what we know. Humanism tells us that man rules above all else, including God. I once saw a quote by Darwin that said, "The more one gets to know oneself, the more godlike one becomes." This mind-set, which permeates our society, leaves God out of the equation in determining behavior and justice. It encourages us to worship the creature (man) more than the creator (God) (Romans 1:25).

Marching Orders

The battle began for you—"the rest of her offspring"—the day you joined God's army. You headed straight into the war zone between the two kingdoms: one headed by God, the other by Satan. One day, God's soldiers will come off the field and go to live forever in heaven, and Satan's kingdom will be overthrown and cast into hell. In the meantime, we remain under enemy occupation. We have work to do and territory to win. Until the day we go to be with Christ, we will continue to be caught in the war between the carnal man and the spiritual one. And though we know that Jesus has won the war at Calvary, we often let Satan, the defeated foe, get the upper hand and defeat us in battle.

My mother's pastor once spent an evening in the Arizona desert, where he came upon a diamondback rattlesnake. He killed the snake and cut off its head. As he carried it back to his truck, the snake continued to shake its rattler and lunge at him. "What's worse," the pastor said, "even though I knew its head was cut off, I still flinched."

We allow Satan to convince us that his lies are truth. Ed Silvoso of Harvest House Ministries defines a stronghold: "A mind-set impregnated with hopelessness, that causes us to see as unchangeable, something that's contrary to the Word of God." When we get something untrue stuck in our minds and think it will never change, we call that a stronghold. Satan works overtime on us to make us lose hope and forfeit our power in Christ. Consequently, we continue to struggle in vulnerable areas. But we can memorize scriptures such as:

> How can anyone enter a strong man's house and carry off his possessions unless he first ties up the strong man? Then he can rob his house. (Matthew 12:29)

> Lest Satan should get an advantage of us: for we are not ignorant of his devices. (2 Corinthians 2:11 KJV)

> Satan has asked to sift you as wheat. But I have prayed for you, Simon, that your faith may not fail. And when you have turned back, strengthen your brothers. (Luke 22:31–32)

Satan still roars, because he knows he's defeated and his time is short. You and I can stand because we, too, know Satan is defeated and his time is short. We can rehearse the end of the story. We can sing praises to the One who ultimately holds the keys to hell and death. And in God's strength we can go about our lives doing what comes next. But what about the damages already done?

Application

My mother makes delicious yeast rolls. She brings them to every family and church gathering, and they are always one of the highlights of the meal. Several years ago, I tried to make these rolls. I followed her recipe to the teaspoon, but they tasted like rocks. I got some advice from my mother and tried again, only to face similar results. So when she came to visit, I watched over her shoulder and took notes. Shortly after she left, I tried the recipe again. I don't remember what else I served for that meal, but I do remember my rolls were delicious, as have been the batches since. I experienced an Aha! moment when I realized, I can do this.

In *The Structure of Scientific Revolutions* (University of Chicago Press, 1996), Thomas Kuhn uses the term "paradigm shift." He defines a paradigm as "our theory, perception, way we see and understand." We see everything according to our mental maps. You look at the wrong map, you get to the wrong place. Shifting our paradigms requires looking at something in a different way. For instance, we are not controlled by our feelings or circumstances or environment; instead, our lives are a function of our behavior. We are not victims, and we can make necessary changes.

We can do the same with our life stories. Part of the beauty of story is the ability we have to revise it, and we do this by shifting our paradigms. As I drove one evening to teach a class at a nearby college, I was inspired by the blooming honey locust trees I spied along the way. Driving down the interstate, I scribbled the basics of a children's story on the back of a bank deposit slip. I brought my masterpiece home and typed it into the computer, then I worked to revise it until I felt it was ready to share with others. And share I did, beginning in my children's classrooms. I sat on a tree stump I brought with me and told the story I had written, revised, and rewritten. I shared not only my story with these young students, but also my revision process.

Your story and mine are still in process. We now know the origin of our conflicts, and we know the happy ending that awaits all of us who trust in Jesus as our personal Savior. But in between, things happen that cause us to forget the beginning and end of the larger story, forcing us to live our current story in a less-than-victorious way. We live as victims, taking the rough knocks handed to us and failing to accept the power to change. We think what's done is done and decide things will never change. But realize this: You may not have had a say in much of your past, but you can take control of your future. Just as I revised the chapters in my book, we can look at parts of our stories that need to be changed and make them new, amended, and improved.

Tiara realized she could revise her story. Born to a never-married, non-Christian mom, Tiara experienced sexual abuse until the age of twelve, as the result of her mother's promiscuity. Then her mother accepted Christ. The promiscuity ended but the abuse didn't. Tiara suffered at the hands of her cousin for the next four years. All this could have prevented Tiara from moving on, but it didn't.

She committed her life to Christ, graduated from high school at the top of her class, and won a four-year scholarship in journalism to a prominent Christian college. After graduation, she accepted a position as an associate magazine editor, and today she works at a major magazine in New York City—while she spreads the good news of Jesus.

So where do people like Tiara—or you—begin to make needed changes?

Examine the Past

As we know, our stories include many parts we had nothing to do with, such as settings into which we were born, in the bigger story as well as the smaller one. Some chapters involve characters who have committed unspeakable atrocities. Others include parts we'd rather forget because of the mistakes we made. I have encountered countless people who have gotten stuck in those chapters, and they find it impossible to move on to a newer, better future.

Despite the pre-Fall condition and what happened after the Fall, salvation offers redemption to all those who would dare to switch their paradigms and revise their stories. Despite the fact that you still live in a human body that continues to decay and gravitate toward evil, through Christ you can be renewed, enlightened, freed from sin, made submissive to God's will, and receive everlasting life.

The way back begins with looking behind at what hurts and honestly surrendering it to God. Then seek supernatural wisdom for a new direction. He may have you go back to school or relocate to a new place or find new friends or just start over where you are today. You can break past curses once and for all, so they won't affect you ever again. I called my mother once to ask her to pray for me, again, about one of those past areas. She said, "Lynda, I've already prayed for that, and I remember the spot on the wall I looked at when I gave it to God."

Mom knew that once something in the past is given to God, healing begins. Then you can look forward to a future with hope; "the hope that He really is what for centuries we have been claiming He is," Frederick Buechner says. "The hope that despite the fact that sin and death still rule the world, He somehow conquered them. The hope that in Him and through him all of us stand a chance of somehow conquering them, too. The hope that at some unforeseeable time and in some unimaginable way, He will return with healing in his wings" (*Wishful Thinking,* HarperSanFrancisco, 1993).

Embrace the Future

When authors make revisions to what they write, they look at past information, decide what needs to be changed, then let the story sit for a while—a process called incubation—and come back to it later to make the desired changes. Sometimes the writer rewords earlier material, as I did when I picked up an old dream and went back to school to earn my doctorate. A rewrite may change the emphasis, and the writer will highlight new events. Sometimes the writer chooses to throw away the whole draft and start over from scratch with a fresh sheet of paper.

But what about the mistakes? I heard the story of a man who went to India to watch the weaving of Persian rugs. He described how the laborers sat in a circle to do their work, with the master weaver squarely in the middle. "What happens when you make a mistake," the man asked. "Do you start over or throw it away?"

"No, we take the error we've made to the master weaver. He studies what we've done, then he carefully redesigns the pattern so it incorporates our mistake into the end design."

But what about the losses I've suffered? For some people, a personal disaster transforms a comedy into a tragedy that they never get over. For others, the tragedy inspires a whole new chapter in their story.

Ann wrote to me from England with the details of how her husband had left her four years before. She had threatened to kill her children, then herself, so her husband wouldn't get custody. Ann and I corresponded for a while, then I arranged to meet her at a London train station on my way back from Paris. I urged her to let go of the past and move on. But she said, "I can't, I hate him." We still stay in touch, and Ann is making some major strides toward healing these days. Meanwhile, the children have suffered along with their mother for the past five years.

My good friend Verdell Davis, on the other hand, took the tragedy of her husband's death in a plane crash, surrendered it to God, and accepted a ministry created from the tragedy. In addition to her book *Let Me Grieve, But Not Forever* (Word Publishing, 1994), Verdell goes throughout the country speaking about loss. She's moving on and looking forward to the next chapters of her life. Her final draft is being written so other people can read and learn from Verdell what she did with the undesirable parts of her life story. How did she handle the conflicts? What themes have emerged? Verdell writes: "Was there meaning in my life solely because of Creath, or was my life with Creath a wonderful bonus to the meaning of my life because of God? So does meaning for me now become impossible because there is no Creath? Or can there be renewed meaning because there is God? I have lost Creath, I haven't lost God. One was a gift in time, the other a gift for eternity."

I heard a story once of a woman who tried to kill herself. After a couple of attempts, her pastor said to her, "If you keep trying, you know you'll succeed. But how are you ever going to stand before God, who loves you so much, and convince Him that His grace wasn't sufficient for you?"

Like Verdell, this woman needed that heart knowledge of 2 Corinthians 12:9–10: "My grace is sufficient for you, for my power is made perfect in weakness." With that knowledge, no matter what she faces, she could "boast all the more gladly about [her] weaknesses, so that Christ's power may rest on [her]. . . . For when [she is] weak, then [she is] strong."

Because of sin, we will always struggle. Because of the Cross, we will always win. Look at the past, then look forward to the future.

Conclusion

Do you want to live the victorious life? During his work with the Navigators, Walter A. Henrichsen wrote: "If you have a big God, you have small problems. If you have a small God, you have big problems. When your God is big, then every seeming problem becomes an opportunity. When your God is small, every problem becomes an obstacle" (*Disciples are Made—Not Born,* Victor Books, 1974).

Because we serve a big God, we can handle big problems and use them as opportunities to lift up the name of Christ. We can hold to the testimony of Jesus and His promise of certain redemption. We can learn His words through the Word, then stand in the face of Satan's onslaughts claiming this truth: "The one who is in you is greater than the one who is in the world" (1 John 4:4).

BIBLE STUDY

Certain rights come with being a child of God. Ultimate victory is guaranteed, and because of Christ, you can revise your own story. You can know your rights and exercise them by answering these questions based on the Word of God:

Who is Satan?

JOHN 10:10: "The __________ comes only to __________ and ______ and ________; I have come that they may have life, and have it to the full."

1 PETER 5:8: "Be self-controlled and alert. Your __________________ the devil prowls around like a __________________ __________________ looking for someone to ____________."

1 JOHN 2:16: "For everything in the world—the __________________ of sinful man, the ___________ of his eyes and the ______________ of what he has and does—comes not from the Father but from the world."

How did Satan originate the drive for self-significance?

ISAIAH 14:12–15: "How you have fallen from heaven, O morning star, son of the dawn! You have been cast down to the earth, you who once laid low the nations! You said in your heart,

'I will ascend to ____________;

I will raise my ______________ above the stars of God;

I will sit ______________ on the mount of assembly, on the utmost heights of the sacred mountain.

I will ascend ______________ the tops of the clouds;

I will make myself like the _______ _________.'

But you are brought down to the grave, to the depths of the pit."

How did the Fall change the following?

Heart and character (Psalm 51:5; Galatians 5:19–21):

Mind (1 Corinthians 2:14; 2 Corinthians 4:3–5; Ephesians 4:17–18):

Conscience (1 Timothy 4:2; Titus 1:15; Hebrews 10:22):

Will (Romans 4:18–19):

Will we always be cursed by the Fall?

ROMANS 8:19–21: "The creation waits in eager expectation for the sons of God to be revealed. For the creation was subjected to __________, not by its own choice, but by the will of the one who subjected it, in hope that the creation itself will be __________ from its bondage to decay and __________ into the glorious freedom of the children of God."

When will we be free?

List some of the ways the enemy has tormented you.

(i.e., robbed you of joy, destroyed your relationships, absorbed you in your own problems so you don't reach out to others).

-
-
-
-

What power do you have over Satan?

COLOSSIANS 1:13–14: "For [God] has rescued us from the dominion of __________ and brought us into the __________ of the _____ he loves, in whom we have ________, the ______________ of _________."

COLOSSIANS 2:15: "And having _________ the powers and authorities, [Christ] made a __________ __________ of them, triumphing over them by the cross."

1 PETER 5:9: "_________ [Satan], standing __________ in the ________, because you know that your __________ throughout the _______ are undergoing the same kind of sufferings."

List some areas where you've allowed Satan to be in charge and you want to take back control today:

-
-
-
-

How do you access power over the enemy?

EPHESIANS 6:10–14: "Be strong in the Lord and in his mighty ________. Put on the ________ ________ of God so that you can take your _______ against the devil's schemes. For our struggle is not against ________ and __________, but against the rulers, against the spiritual forces of _______ in the heavenly realms. Therefore put on the full ________ of _______, so that when the day of _________ comes, you may be able to __________ your ground."

What does the full armor include?

EPHESIANS 6:14–18: "The _________ of __________ buckled around your waist."

"The ______________ of _____________ in place."

"Your feet fitted with the ____________ that comes from the gospel of _________."

"Take up the ______________ of ______________, with which you can extinguish all the flaming _________ of the _______ _______."

"Take the ____________ of _______________ and the sword of the __________, which is the __________ of ___________."

"And _____________ in the Spirit on all occasions with all kinds of prayers and ____________."

Truth, righteousness, peace, faith, the word of God, and prayer: these constitute our armor.

What are the steps to victory over the enemy?

Confess your sins. Ask God to forgive you for believing Satan's lies.

1 JOHN 1:9: "If we _________ our sins, [God] is ____________ and __________ and will ___________ us our sins and purify us from all _______________."

Take back what's been stolen from you. When you give ground to the enemy, you give him permission to build a stronghold out of the lies he tells you (John 8:44). You give him the keys to your house. Take back the ground you've surrendered to the enemy; "and do not give the devil a ______________. He who has been ____________ must steal no longer" (Ephesians 4:27–28).

Refute the lies. Tear down strongholds. Remember, Satan, who deceives the whole world, was cast out of heaven (Revelation 12:9).

JOHN 8:32: "Then you will know the __________, and the ___________ will set you __________."

ROMANS 12:2: "Do not _______________ any longer to the pattern of this ________, but be _______________ by the ______________ of your _________. Then you will be able to test and approve what God's will is—his good, pleasing and perfect will."

Embrace the truth. Reprogram your mind about you, God, and Satan. The Bible supplies the truth that replaces the lies. You can run to it for safety and victory.

PSALM 18:2–3: "The LORD is my __________, my __________ and my _________; my God is my rock, in whom I take refuge. . . . I call to the LORD, who is worthy of praise, and I am saved from my enemies."

PROVERBS 18:10: "The name of the LORD is a __________ _________; the righteous run to it and are __________."

Renew your mind. As we have seen, the mind is the battleground for spiritual warfare.

2 CORINTHIANS 10:5: "We demolish _____________ and every _______________ that sets itself up against the _____________ of God, and we take ________________ every ______________ to make it _____________ to Christ."

PHILIPPIANS 4:8: "Whatever is true, whatever is noble, whatever is right, whatever is pure, whatever is lovely, whatever is admirable—if anything is excellent or praiseworthy—think about such things."

HEBREWS 12:1: "Let us throw off everything that hinders and the sin that so easily _________, and let us run with _______________ the race marked out for us."

JAMES 4:7: "Submit yourselves, then, to God. _________ the ___________, and he will flee from you."

Dear God:

Thanks for my Aha! moment. I now realize my victory over the enemy. I am a joint heir with Your Son, Jesus. That makes me Mary's other offspring and a target for Satan's attacks. Thanks for the provision

You give me to write my future regardless of the past. "In all these things we are more than conquerors through him who loved us." I can recognize strongholds and pull them down because I have power over the enemy. Jesus, when You died on the cross and said, "It is finished," everything became new. You revised the story. And because of my faith in You, I can live a new life. In the name of Jesus Christ, amen.

CHAPTER 3

I Am Loved

Embracing the Bigger Story

"For God so loved the world that he gave his one and only Son, that whoever believes in him shall not perish but have eternal life."

—JOHN 3:16

His name was J. T. Bryson—Brother Bryson to us. He lived in Kingston, Jamaica, but when he came to the U.S. to speak at my father's church, he always stayed in our home. I was in elementary school during those years, and though I was taller than most of the children in my class, Brother Bryson seemed like a giant to me. His dark skin stretched over his nearly seven-foot frame and contrasted against his white teeth, which were seen often through his steady laughter. His riddles and stories almost always included us children. And one tale stands out most clearly in my mind.

There was once a little boy who built a boat, and it was his most prized possession. He took the boat out to the river to see if its majestic appearance would be matched by its ability to sail. And sail it did. It moved away from the shore so quickly that it stretched beyond the boy's reach and soon sailed out of sight. The boy returned home in tears; his prize gone, his hard work in vain.

One day the little boy walked down the street, his hands stuck in his pockets. Suddenly he saw his boat displayed in a store window. The boy couldn't move quickly enough as he opened the heavy door and ran to the counter. Out of breath he said, "My boat! You found my boat! May I please have back the boat I made?"

"Two dollars. That's the price. Give me two dollars, son, and the boat is yours," the clerk said.

The boy ran out of the store and back home. He counted his pennies, but it wasn't enough. He performed odd jobs for his mother and their neighbor over the next few days. Finally he counted: $1.98, $1.99, $2.00. Without a word, he ran out the door. The boy laid two dollars in change on the counter, and the clerk handed over the boat. The boy clutched it to his chest and said, "Little boat, little boat, twice I have loved you. First I made you, now I bought you."

Perhaps it was just the attention Brother Bryson paid to me, one of the eight Hunter kids, but something in that story rang dear to me. I longed to know how much God loved just me, Lynda. At times I felt no one loved me at all. Many of you feel the same way, especially if you've never experienced unconditional love or if someone for whom you cared deeply betrayed you.

After I surrendered my life to God—though pregnant, alone, and uncertain about the future—I began to feel good about myself for the first time in my life. Once I saw me as God sees me, I began the process of learning who I was to Him: loved, accepted, and forgiven. I remember standing in front of the mirror once when I had no one to look pretty for and saying, "How do I look to you today, Lord?" When I felt down, I'd picture myself crawling into His lap and having Him play with my hair. Eventually, this new confidence freed me from self–preoccupation and allowed me to look outward to other people and to the work He'd called me to do.

God's great love for you and me is the reason for our significance. Because that irretractable love reaches so far, no one can take it away from us, and no one can take away our God-significance either. It's a done deal. Sealed on Calvary, a nonnegotiable item. One of the first Christian songs we learn as children is "Jesus Loves Me, This I Know." It's time we learn that truth. After all, it's only because of the larger story that we can make sense of our individual stories.

Scripture

Mephibosheth had many reasons to struggle with God's love and his own significance. His grandfather, King Saul, had grown jealous of David, who'd been anointed to replace him as the second king of Israel. To make matters worse, Saul's oldest son, Jonathan, loved the former shepherd boy, despite the fact that Jonathan was heir apparent to the throne. Jonathan even stripped himself of his own royal regalia and placed it on David in recognition of his divine election to be king (1 Samuel 18:4). And there was covenant between them (1 Samuel 18:3).

Covenant—an agreement between two parties—comes from the root word in Hebrew meaning "to cut." In his book *The Covenant* (Beacon Hill Press, 1999), James L. Garlow described several ceremonial steps that occur between the parties of a covenant before witnesses:

- Exchanging robes, representing an exchange of identity
- Exchanging belts, representing an exchange of strengths and assets
- Exchanging weapons, representing an exchange of enemies
- Marking the body, usually the wrists, and mingling the blood. The tradition of waving and shaking hands is said to have originated from this ceremony, which showed others the party to be in covenant with someone else.

- Sacrificing, by slicing a heifer down the underside of the belly and folding out. Hence, the "blood covenant."
- Taking the "walk of death" through the bloody sacrifice
- Pronouncing blessings for terms kept and curses for breaking terms
- Sharing a covenant meal
- Exchanging names, representing the merging of identities

David became so effective with his military tactics that his exploits were celebrated in song: "Saul has slain his thousands, and David his tens of thousands" (1 Samuel 18:7). So jealous Saul set out to kill David. And he tried—twenty-one times. Jonathan sought to bring his father and his friend to a meeting of the minds, but it didn't happen. And because of the covenant he had cut with David, Jonathan protected his friend rather than siding with his father. Covenant superseded every other relationship.

David had to flee for his life, and he reminded Jonathan of their covenant: "As for you, show kindness to your servant, for you have brought him into a covenant with you before the LORD" (1 Samuel 20:8).

Jonathan stood by David because of their blood bond. Then Saul and Jonathan were killed in battle. Saul's household panicked at David's possible wrath. So a nurse ran away with Jonathan's oldest son, five-year-old Mephibosheth, who stood next in line for the throne. While running with Mephibosheth, the nurse fell and crippled him (2 Samuel 4:4). The boy grew up in a place outside King David's jurisdiction called Lo-debar, meaning "not a pasture." Every day the young man lived in that barren land, and his crippled leg probably reminded him of his lost crown and the bad blood between him and the king.

Many years passed. One day Mephibosheth received a summons to appear before King David. He must have trembled as he received the call. His life had been one of insignificance and sadness. *What will the king do to me?* he must have wondered.

What Mephibosheth didn't know is that his dad had made a covenant with David. He didn't know that Jonathan had willingly sacrificed the throne and risked his own life to save David's. Mephibosheth also didn't know that David still loved Jonathan and had said, "Is there anyone still left of the house of Saul to whom I can show kindness for Jonathan's sake?" (2 Samuel 9:1).

Mephibosheth stood before the king and he soon learned what had been in store for him all along because of his father's covenant. "'Don't be afraid,' David said to him, 'for I will surely show you kindness for the sake of your father Jonathan. I will restore to you all the land that belonged to your grandfather Saul, and you will always eat at my table'" (2 Samuel 9:7).

The Old Covenant—and the New

Why did God love Mephibosheth so much? Because of covenant. Why does He love you and me? Because of covenant. God's sovereign plan in history came through His covenant with a man called Abraham (Abram, as he was originally known). A Semite (descendant of Noah's son Shem, as seen in Genesis 11:21–31), he was the first person in the Bible to be called a Hebrew (Genesis 14:13). All Jews trace their ancestry to Abraham, the father of their nation.

We read in the first few verses of Genesis 12 the call God gave to Abraham. He went on to promise Abraham that his offspring would inherit Canaan (13:14; 17:8); he would have many descendants (13:16; 15:5); and all people would be blessed through him (12:3).

In the New Testament, Peter's speech to fellow Jews gathered near the Temple indicates that they, as physical descendants of Abraham, are heirs of this promised blessing (Acts 3:12, 25). But the New Testament also indicates that Gentile believers—those who are spiritual rather than lineal descendants of Abraham—likewise share in Abraham's kinship (Galatians 3:7–8). All Christians find their origin in Abraham the Hebrew: "If you belong to Christ, then you are Abraham's seed" (Galatians 3:29).

Back in Genesis 17:5, God told Abraham, "I have made you a father of many nations." The Hebrew word translated "nations" is *goyim,* which can be translated "Gentile." This means that God's covenant sphere would be enlarged, and that non-Jews would one day name Abraham as their father too. Paul says that Abraham's spiritual family includes those who share the faith of Abraham, for he's "the father of all who believe" (Romans 4:11).

That means me. And I have witnessed God's love for me through His covenant on more than one occasion. One Saturday before Christmas, I took my children to Denver to go shopping. One of my children had been struggling with her faith, and I wanted to help her through, but I felt discouraged and increasingly helpless to assist her search. My fearfulness and frustration grew as the day wore on. When we arrived home and plugged in the Christmas tree lights, I felt the last straw fall when the lights wouldn't come on.

I went to bed and poured out my heart to God. That night, I had a dream that a man phoned me. He asked me how things were going, and I told him—even about the Christmas lights. He instructed me to go to the copy machine, remove the cord, and plug it into the tree at a specific place.

The next morning, I rose early, took a shower, and went to my office to spend time reading my Bible. I glanced at the copy machine and remembered my dream. Curiosity got the best of me, and I removed the cord and plugged it into the tree in the family room just where the man had told me to. The tree was immediately ablaze with white lights.

I looked out over the snow in the backyard as I ate my oatmeal, thanking God that even my Christmas tree was important to Him. *Consider the lilies,* I felt Him say to my heart. I reread the Matthew 6 passage and realized the disciples weren't asking Jesus *about* the lilies. They were asking, instead, about what they'd eat and drink, and maybe even about their teenage kids. But Jesus *gave* them the lilies to hold in their hands so they could also believe in the things that they couldn't hold.

I had experienced God's love for me in the practical, everyday places of life. And once again, I understood that no one could ever take that away from me.

Application

The word "covenant" in its Hebrew form is used nearly three hundred times in the Bible. It is not clearly defined in Scripture because the people of that time simply understood its meaning and importance. To the Hebrew mind, the idea of covenant covered all kinds of human relationships. It represented a bond that united people in mutual obligation, whether through a marriage contract, a commercial enterprise, or a verbal undertaking. The word "testament," as used in the titles of the Old and New Testament, has the same meaning. It was only natural that people's relationship to God would also be expressed in terms of the covenant.

The closest tradition we have in Western culture to the covenant ceremony is the wedding. The essence of marriage is covenant. God chides Israel for not being faithful to the "wife of your marriage covenant" (Malachi 2:14). In the allegory of God's covenant bonding to his chosen people, he says, "I passed by, and . . . saw that you were old enough for love. . . . I gave you my solemn oath and entered into a covenant with you, . . . and you became mine" (Ezekiel 16:8). Then Proverbs 2:17 warns of a woman "who has left the partner of her youth and ignored the covenant she made before God."

Rabbis regarded the Jewish marriage service as reflective of the main features of God's covenant with Israel at Mt. Sinai. The Bible likens God to a bridegroom and the Hebrew people to His bride (Isaiah 54:5–6; 62:5). The Lord says through Jeremiah that when His new covenant is established some day, "It will not be like the covenant I made with their forefathers when I took them by the hand to lead them out of Egypt, because they broke my covenant, though I was a husband to them" (Jeremiah 31:32). God also says to His people Israel that "you will call me 'my husband'" (Hosea 2:16).

A wife reinforces her love for her husband by upholding their wedding vows. God wants you and me to reinforce our love for Him by upholding our vows too. By bringing His covenant down to where we live and likening it to a marriage contract with Him, we remember what that commitment means:

I am set apart. The first part of the Jewish marriage ceremony, which contractually sets the couple aside in betrothal, is known as *kiddushin.* It involves an act of sanctification or consecration. It means to "be set apart" or "to be holy." So marriage is an act of being set apart unto God and each other. Before the law was given, God said to Moses, "Go to the people and consecrate them" (Exodus 19:10). Living a life of holiness means setting ourselves apart; looking, talking, acting, and responding differently than the world. This happens by bringing our weaknesses—anything not like Christ—before God and surrendering them to His control.

I am under a marriage contract. The *ketubah* is the marriage contract detailing the obligations and terms of the union, and it is read to the bride before she makes her final commitment to the bridegroom. Just as the *ketubah* stipulated the conditions for the marriage, so the binding on Sinai detailed the divine stipulations in covenant formula (Exodus 19:5, 7–8). The Bible is our marriage contract. When we enter into covenant with God by giving our lives to Him, we agree to the terms of His Word. It becomes the true north in the compass of our behavior and for any decisions we make.

I will uphold the permanence of my marriage covenant. If one attempts to break the marriage covenant, the blood serves as a powerful visual lesson that one's own blood will be shed, making it inviolable and irrevocable. God's covenant with Israel is everlasting (Genesis 17:7). To Israel he said, "I will betroth you to me forever" (Hosea 2:19). God engraves Israel on the palms of His hands (Isaiah 49:16) and pledges that His covenant loyalty will be as constant as the shining of the sun, moon, and stars (Jeremiah 31:35–36). Though divorce has become an acceptable course of action to modern-day marriage vows, divorce must never be an option to one who gives her life to Christ. She will never "change her mind" about her commitment to her Husband.

I will uphold the exclusivity of my marriage commitment. The marriage commitment rules out potential rivals who might compete for the attention of a marriage partner. On Mt. Sinai, God said, "You shall have no other gods before me" (Exodus 20:3), and in Exodus 20:5, God calls Himself a jealous God. Other gods that would come between you and God can be a busy schedule or your husband, your children or your job—anything that takes you away from regular time and devotion to Him. These things become the gods that mess up the exclusivity of your marriage commitment.

I will keep my promise. At Sinai, Israel pledged publicly their agreement to the terms of the covenant (Exodus 19:7–8). One's word was equal to one's promise (Psalm 15:4). "For better or for worse," are the words in the natural marriage covenant. You must also agree to serve the Lord with your whole heart and for your whole life, in the good times as well as the bad.

I will periodically renew my vows. The covenant of marriage should be renewed. God's covenant with Abraham did not end with Abraham. The Davidic Covenant (2 Samuel 7) restated and enriched the Sinaitic Covenant. The New Covenant established through the blood of Jesus, became the final and fullest expression of God's covenant love (Luke 22:20; 1 Corinthians 11:25). David asked God to restore to him the joy of His salvation (Psalm 51:12). He was asking to renew his marriage vows with God, to make that day as exciting as when he first fell in love with his Lord.

Today the emotion of the moment causes us to forget our pledge to each other. We need to be reminded of our marriage vows. Disobedience means forfeiting the personal benefits and blessings that accrue only through faithfulness. We get out of our marriage what we invest in it. Periodic renewal of the vows keeps us aware of how our investment is doing.

I am living in the preparation time. Marriage is no spur-of-the-moment, serendipitous encounter. A betrothal period is set aside as a time of preparation. Scripture designates the church as Christ's bride (Ephesians 5:25–32; Revelation 19:7). She is to prepare herself for the wedding, which is to be a time of celebration. Then, in the Jewish community, the bride and bridegroom make their way to the wedding canopy, accompanied by attendants carrying candles. This practice parallels the parable of the ten virgins (Matthew 25:1–13). We should do everything to be prepared to be with Him today, though we may still have lots of tomorrows.

I will meet my waiting groom, God, one day. In a Jewish marriage, the bridegroom comes first to the *huppah* (canopy) where the couple stands throughout the ceremony, and waits there for the coming of the bride. In Scripture, we read, "The LORD came from Sinai and dawned over them from Seir" (Deuteronomy 33:2). Always remember that the One we will meet in the end is the One who has held everything in the palm of His hand since the beginning. That's reason to be ready for your groom.

Jewish tradition teaches in a striking way that the joining of a man and woman in the covenant of marriage is a replica of God's eternal covenant relationship to his chosen. To understand biblical marriage is to understand the biblical concept of covenant.

CONCLUSION

Brother Bryson went to be with the Lord when I was in my early teens. He will never again come and stay in our home or sit with us and laugh this side of heaven. But he left the reminder that goes with me always: "First He made me, then He bought me."

Brother Bryson left behind something else that would stay with me. It was this little chorus he would sing as tears streaked down his brown cheeks:

Iysh, Iysh, He's my jewel,
Mine while endless ages roll.
He's my altogether lovely,
He's the Iysh of my soul.

I loved the song because I loved Brother Bryson, but it would be years before I found myself able to define the One about whom the song was sung. I discovered that *Iysh* meant "great and mighty man, husband," as it says in Isaiah 54:5: "For your Maker is your husband—the LORD Almighty is his name."

BIBLE STUDY

You don't have to live in the barrenness and poverty of Lo-debar. You don't have to live as a cripple. The riches of God's inheritance belong to those who keep His covenant.

Have you felt insignificant before God and others? Have you believed that you can be safe only by hiding from God, shaping your own destiny and taking care of yourself? Have you convinced yourself that your life story will never be any better than it is today?

God made a deal with us through His covenant—one which cannot be broken. And to not realize this, to not take advantage of the covenant blessings, is like having money in the bank and never writing checks on it.

"Know therefore that the LORD your God is God; he is the faithful God, keeping his covenant of love to a thousand generations of those who love him and keep his commands" (Deuteronomy 7:9).

God's love for you

ROMANS 5:8: "But God _______________ his own love for us in this: While we were still _________, Christ ______ for us."

PSALM 18:50: "He shows unfailing _______________ to his _________________."

PSALM 62:12: "You, O Lord, are loving. Surely you will __________ each person according to _____________ he has __________."

MICAH 7:18: "Who is a God like you, who ___________

sin and __________ the transgression of the ____________ of his inheritance?"

ZEPHANIAH 3:17: "The LORD your God is with you, . . . he will _______ you with his love, he will __________ over you with singing."

ROMANS 5:5: "And __________ does not disappoint us, because God has poured out his love into our hearts by the ____________ ______________, whom he has given us."

1 JOHN 3:1: "How great is the love the Father has ________________ on us, that we should be called ______________________ of God! And that is what we are!"

EXODUS 20:6: "But showing love to a thousand generations of those who love me and keep my commandments."

God loves _________ forever and ever and ever.

Characteristics of God's love

JEREMIAH 31:3: "I have loved you with an everlasting love; I have drawn you with loving- _______________."

PSALM 115:1: "Not to us, O LORD, not to us but to your name be the glory, because of your love and ______________."

PSALM 103:8: "The LORD is _________________ and ___________, ________ to _______, abounding in love."

PSALM 85:9–10: "Surely his salvation is ______________ those who ___________ him. . . . Love and _______________ meet together; __________ and __________ kiss each other."

JEREMIAH 31:20: "'Therefore my heart __________ for him; I have great _______________ for him,' declares the Lord."

PSALM 145:9–10: "The Lord is ________ to __________; he has __________ on all he has made."

EPHESIANS 2:4: "But because of his great love for us, God, who is rich in __________, made us alive with Christ."

God's love for me is ______________ and ______________ and ________________ and ________________.

Does He know me well?

For you created my inmost being;
you knit me together in my mother's womb.
I praise you because I am fearfully and wonderfully made; . . .
My frame was not hidden from you
when I was made in the secret place.
When I was woven together in the depths of the earth,
your eyes saw my unformed body.
All the days ordained for me
were written in your book
before one of them came to be.
(Psalm 139:13–16)

God has known ______________ and ________________ and ______________ about me since before I was born.

Our love for God

DEUTERONOMY 6:5: "Love the LORD your God with all your ______ and with all your ___________ and with all your ___________."

DEUTERONOMY 11:1: "Love the Lord your God and keep his ______________, his ________________, his ___________ and his ___________________ always."

PSALM 119:47–48: "For I delight in your ____________ because I love them. I lift up my hands to your commands, which I ____________, and I ________ on your decrees."

JOHN 14:15, 21, 23: "If you love me, you will ____________ what I command. . . . Whoever has my commands and obeys them, he is the one who __________ me. He who loves me will be loved by my Father, and I too will love him and ____________ myself to him. . . . If anyone loves me, he will obey my ____________. My Father will love him, and we will come to him and make our ____________ with him. He who does not love me will not obey my teaching. These words you hear are not my own; they belong to the ____________ who sent me."

I can show my love back to God by ______________, ______________, and ___________.

What can separate us from God's love?

ROMANS 8:35–39: "Who shall separate us from the love of Christ? Shall trouble or hardship or persecution or famine or nakedness or danger or sword? . . . No, in all these things we are more than conquerors through him who loved us. For I am convinced that neither death nor life, neither angels nor demons, neither the present nor the future, nor any powers, neither height nor depth, nor anything else in all creation, will be able to separate us from the love of God that is in Christ Jesus our Lord."

________________________ can separate us from God's love.

_________________________ can separate us from God-significance.

Dear God:

You love me so much that You gave Your one and only Son, so I could believe in You and have eternal life. Never again will I believe that I am not loved. What an incredible truth that no one can ever take that away from me! To show my gratitude, I will uphold my covenant commitment with You by keeping your commands and teachings. I will live for You all my life. Thank you giving your one and only Son. Thank you that I believe in You and will have eternal life. In the name of Jesus Christ, amen.

CHAPTER 4

I Am Free

Overcoming Conflicts in Your Story

"If the Son sets you free,
you will be free indeed."

—JOHN 8:36

Debbie was born to a prostitute drug addict and abandoned in the hospital at birth. Her grandmother picked her up at the hospital and raised her until shortly after Debbie's twelfth birthday, when her grandmother died. An aunt and uncle took Debbie home with them, and her uncle immediately began to abuse her sexually. She found a boyfriend when she turned fourteen who died in a drive-by shooting, but not before Debbie learned she was pregnant.

Her uncle's child was born when Debbie was fifteen, and the state removed both mother and child from the relatives' care. Debbie and her daughter bounced from foster home to foster home. At the age of nineteen, she met a man in the service who offered to take care of her. She married him, experienced extensive physical and emotional abuse, and divorced him after seven years of marriage. Debbie is now thirty-one years old, and during the three years I have known her, she has lived with three different men and farmed out her now-fifteen-year-old daughter to live with friends.

Debbie loathes her past, yet in many ways she seems bent on repeating it. She hates the fact that her mother prostituted herself, yet she lives with man after man—not for money, but for companionship and a roof over her head. Debbie resents that her mother dropped out of her life, yet she repeatedly gives her daughter away and remains emotionally distant. Her daughter now finds herself almost grown with no more of a clue about how to do life than her mother before her.

Just about the time we think we've been handed a raw deal in life, we meet someone like Debbie, who has experiences that almost defy description. All of us come with a history, previous chapters that led up to the events of today. Some of us look squarely at the past, gain a healthy understanding of what went wrong, and make efforts to change things in the future. Others of us, like Debbie, can't seem to break from past curses.

So what do we do with the things that have previously defined us? Are you one who says, "I can't get over what's happened to me," or do you say, "I am free from my past"?

Every story includes conflicts, which fall into one of three categories: man vs. man, man vs. nature, or man vs. self. Your story and mine also feature conflicts. We read about them in James 1:2: "Consider it pure joy, my brothers, whenever you face trials [conflicts] of many kinds." Not "if you face," but, "whenever you face." Like Debbie, we may have experienced insufferable injustices at the hand of someone else. Others of us found ourselves born into unspeakable circumstances, or we encountered accidents that forever altered our way of life. Still others of us deal daily with the consequences of mistakes we've made. Whether the source of the conflict comes from others, nature, or self, we can remain tethered to the past. But there's another option, to "consider it pure joy" when we face conflicts, and this option allows us to move on to a promising tomorrow. Men and women since the beginning of time have found that God majors in making things new and in enabling joy, though He never wastes experiences that have already happened. He knows and uses even the bad things for His glory, and as a way for us to get to know Him better. We find evidence of that kind of work in the story of a woman in Samaria.

Scripture

Jesus had been in Judea, then he headed for Galilee. But the Bible said, "He had to go through Samaria" (John 4:4). He had a job to do there. When He arrived in the town of Sychar, he sat down by a well to rest at about six o'clock in the evening.

Up walked a Samaritan woman, and Jesus asked her for a drink.

HE: "If you knew the gift of God and who it is that asks you for a drink, you would have asked him and he would have given you living water" (v. 10).

SHE: "Where can you get this living water?" (v. 11).

HE: "Everyone who drinks this water will be thirsty again, but whoever drinks the water I give him will never thirst. Indeed, the water I give him will become in him a spring of water welling up to eternal life" (v. 13–14).

SHE: (still not getting it) Wow! Tell me how to get it so I won't have to come to this well.

HE: (changing the subject to the important things) Go get your husband.

SHE: I don't have a husband.

HE: You're right. You have had five husbands, and the man you live with now is not your husband. God is spirit, and his worshipers must worship in spirit and in truth.

SHE: (still not recognizing Him) I know the Messiah is coming. When He does, He'll explain all this to us.

HE: I who speak to you am He.

Why did Jesus go out of His way to reach this woman? A well-known early Jewish prayer shows the disdain and prejudice people held at that time: "Blessed art thou, O Lord . . . who has not made me Samaritan or woman." Yet the person Jesus made a special point to see was both!

THE WOMAN'S PAST

Samaria was the shortest route between Judea and Galilee, but not the only way. Jesus could have gone through Perea, east of the Jordan River, the route the Jews normally chose because of their hatred of the Samaritans.

After Samaria fell to Assyria in 722 B.C., Israelites and Assyrians intermarried. Their descendants, the Samaritans, were regarded by the Jews as neither fully Jew nor fully Gentile because they had adopted Israel's religion and combined it with their own polytheism. Over a long period of time, the Jews came to hate the Samaritans. That's why the disciples found what Jesus did so shocking.

Jesus chose the route through a place usually avoided at all costs. Then "his disciples returned and were surprised to find him talking with a woman" (John 4:27). When Jesus asked the Samaritan woman for a drink, she said, "You are a Jew and I am a Samaritan woman. How can you ask me for a drink?" (v. 9).

This unnamed women knew that, as a patriarchal society, Israel did not deem women as equal in importance to men. This sentiment led to abuses by some men and laws, which restricted women in their activities, legal functions, and significance.

- Only men could own property, unless there were not sons (Numbers 27:8).

- A wife could keep a pledge only if her husband agreed to allow her (Numbers 30:10–12).
- When a woman failed to have a child, it was assumed to be her problem and an expression of disapproval by God (Genesis 30:1–2, 22).
- A woman was expected to prove her virginity (Deuteronomy 22:20), but men were not.
- A woman's life was considered to have half the monetary value of a man's (Leviticus 27:1–8).
- Most women moved unquestioningly into marriage, and those who did not, remained under their father's authority and protection.

In this society, parents hoped for boy babies rather than girls. That feeling added greatly to limiting the value of women.

Then Along Came Jesus

Jesus crossed social barriers and maintained a vital ministry among the forsaken gender:

He kept women close. Orthodox Jews excluded women from worship and kept them in the rear of the synagogue. But Jesus ignored the antiwomen feelings and instituted a program of involvement for women. Everyone, including women, had full access to God.

He taught women. Jesus taught some of his most profound concepts to women, usually in private, as He did with the woman at the well. He also taught publicly to mixed audiences.

He met with women in public. During times of festivals, women were expected to stay inside. It was presumed inappropriate for educated men to talk with women in public, sometimes even their own wives. But Jesus did.

He allowed women to touch him. He healed the woman with the issue of blood in Mark 5, after she touched the hem of his cloak.

He attracted prostitutes. Jesus did not condone their activity, but He did sympathize with the people. The Pharisees believed they should be given no help. But Jesus preferred to minister to promiscuous women such as the Samaritan woman rather than to cold-hearted religionists who were too rigid to listen to God.

As a Result . . .

After her encounter with Jesus, the Samaritan woman, "leaving her water jar," went back to the town and told the people, "Come, see a man who told me everything I ever did. Could this be the Christ?" (John 4:28–29).

The people came out of the town and made their way toward Jesus. "Many of the Samaritans from that town believed in him because of the woman's testimony, 'He told me everything I ever did'" (John 4:39). As the people spent time listening to Jesus for themselves, they said to the woman, "We no longer believe just because of what you said; now we have heard for ourselves, and we know that this man really is the Savior of the world" (John 4:42).

Because of Jesus, things changed for the woman. The Samaritan woman left her past and her struggles with self-worth behind—the water jar—and went on to a new life of more important things. Not only did Jesus' touch in her life help the woman, but she immediately went to work leading others to Him. As a result, their lives were changed as well.

APPLICATION

The Samaritan woman held a track record similar to Debbie's, and nothing seemed as if it would change. In addition to the fact that she was born into inferior status as a Samaritan, what else had happened to affect the way she felt about herself? The Bible doesn't provide information about her growing-up years, but they undoubtedly played a part in her adult life. Jesus began healing the woman by having her face what had happened to her. We can do the same by taking a look at our early years and how they affected our feelings of significance. In his book *The Sensation of Being Somebody* (Zondervan, 1975), Maurice Wagner says our sense of self emerges from three areas:

WORTH

The sense of worth involves excellence, merit, perfection, quality, virtue, usefulness, and importance. A woman with a strong sense of worth feels affirmed and cherished as a person of value. A poor sense of worth makes a person feel inadequate, unuseful, and unimportant.

Self-worth is one of the earliest formed and most complex responses, and it continually reshapes itself over the course of a human life. By age one, a child recognizes that a mirror image of herself is not another person. A rudimentary sense of self comes a few months later, though this image stops at the boundaries of her physical body in the early years.

Then the child develops special relationships with other people and things, which become possessions and extensions of herself. Anything that happens to those self-extensions appears to happen to the child herself. That's why suffering sexual abuse at the hands of someone the child trusts can affect her so deeply. That's also why the child often blames herself for major changes in the home, such as divorce or an accident. If someone demeans the child's worth, that lack of worth becomes fact to the child. If she receives a positive message from her environment, she thinks positively of herself as well.

Tonya grew up in the Italian culture based in the southern part of the United States. She was taught as a child that her people were a superior race, faithful, and virtuous. As Tonya began to discover the truth about her father's infidelities and other mistakes different family members had made, she turned to food to console herself, and she began to gain weight. In a child's early years, satisfaction with the body is closely related to satisfaction with self. Tonya learned to judge herself based on her body's appearance, and a broader inferiority complex resulted.

Children like Tonya try to compensate for dissatisfaction with their bodies and their sense of worth by manipulating their bodies and striving for superiority in other areas. Eating disorders and fitness obsessions often result. The child learns early that a strong identity comes as the result of feeling at home in one's body. It gives a sense of knowing where she is going, and an inner assuredness of approval from people who matter. This idea is reinforced when the child hears comments such as, "You look good, honey. Dropped some weight there?" And so the experience continues, greatly affecting the formation of her self-worth into adolescence.

Belonging

The sense of belonging involves the person's fit, match, place, or function as part of something else. It means having a sense of security and identity with others who love, accept, and support that person. It involves feeling safe, cared for, and sheltered. Identity includes feelings of kinship, likeness, sameness, and oneness. A poor sense of belonging causes the person to feel insecure, unsafe, threatened, unsupported, alone, anxious, and fearful of new experiences.

The person then lacks identity, feels different, unequal, and distant from those who love her.

Finding a healthy sense of belonging gets harder in the adolescent years. Like a trapeze artist, a girl must release her hold on childhood and the familiar and reach in midair for a firm grasp on adulthood and the unfamiliar. The search for identity intensifies with the collision of rapid physical changes and the need to make some adult decisions.

As a result of trying on various roles and struggling with the sense of self, many adolescents develop a blurred self-image and sense of significance. "Who am I?" "Where do I belong?" "Where am I going?" The adolescent asks these questions for the first time before she has the tools or experience to answer them properly. This ambiguity and lack of foundation leads many adolescents to identity diffusion—over-commitment to cliques, allegiances, loves, and social causes. As a result of conflicting feelings, she may develop a lifestyle at odds with the way she was raised. That's why we see so much rebellion during the adolescent years in our society.

Haley relocated with her parents and one sister to another state when her father was transferred. She went from an elementary sixth grade at the top of her class academically and socially, to the last three weeks of a junior-high sixth grade where she felt she was a nobody. After the first day of school, she came home unable to talk. Everything new, including sports involvement, left Haley wondering more than ever where she belonged, and she began doing whatever she found necessary in her quest to fit in. By the next fall, her decisions had affected her whole family, sending her Christian home into a three-year period of turmoil.

Most sociologists and anthropologists tell us that few people make the transition from childhood to adulthood with more difficulty than do those in Western nations. At adolescence, boys and girls are expected to stop being children, yet they are not expected to be adults. They are no longer children, but they are still treated like dependents and are frequently viewed by society as untrustworthy and irresponsible. As a result, conflicting expectations generate an especially intense identity crisis among youth in the U. S. and Europe.

Some non-Western societies, on the other hand, make the period of adolescence easier and more definitive. They ease the shift in status by proving puberty rites—initiation ceremonies that socially symbolize the transition from childhood to adulthood. Adolescents are subjected to distasteful, painful, and humiliating experiences during such ceremonies, after which they are pronounced adults. Boys may be terrorized, ritualistically painted, and circumcised; girls may be secluded. But the tasks are clearly defined, and young people know that if they accomplish the goals set for them, they will acquire adult status, accountability, and responsibility for themselves. This provides an institutional means of easing the transition from youth to adulthood.

In our culture, however, the absorption of the adolescent with her inadequacies robs her of the ability to relate to others—especially with people who remind her of her shortcomings or those whose judgment she values and wants to influence. The adolescent's reaction to these situations portrays her as uncaring, proud, and egocentric, and prevents her from receiving the love and acceptance she so desperately needs. Haley told me once, "I cuss someone out and look the hard part, then I run to my room and cry myself to sleep."

The absence of absolute values further compounds the problem of growing up in this day and time. While teaching at a secular university, one of my students in an issues class once said, "I've been told I shouldn't cheat, but no one ever told me why." At that same university, I learned not to sling the term "values" around unless I was prepared to hear a plethora of voices ask, "Whose values?"

The experiences you encountered and the help (or lack of) you had navigating through them largely determined how you arrived into adulthood, and whether or not you have a healthy sense of self and belonging.

COMPETENCE

The sense of competence includes capability and the feelings of adequacy, sufficiency, and qualifiedness. A low sense of competence renders a woman inadequate, incapable, and unable to achieve a desired goal.

According to a recent survey of three thousand youngsters commissioned by the American Association of University Women, women emerge from adolescence with poorer self-images, relatively lower expectations for life, and less confidence in themselves and their abilities than do men. During their elementary school years, most girls exhibit confidence, assertiveness, and positive feelings about themselves. But by the time they reach high school, less than a third still feel this way. Boys also lose some measure of self-worth, but they end up ahead of the girls.

Many adults perceive themselves according to a picture formed early in life more than by their accomplishments as adults. Many of these individuals who are outwardly successful are constantly depressed and anxious inside because of the poor sense of competence they developed in childhood. In crisis, that inadequate undergirding of their competence becomes evident.

A person who has a healthy sense of her own significance also has a healthy sense of self-worth, belonging, and competence. She uses her potential to achieve goals. She feels adequate, capable, qualified, fit for the job, and equipped with ample resources. But to emerge into adulthood with these areas intact is nearly impossible without God. Even with God, many variables continue to fight against us and the significance we hold. It requires the deliberate decision to meet Jesus at the well, talk with Him there about our pasts, then allowing Him to help us leave our water jars behind and tell our world about Jesus.

CONCLUSION

When I became a single mom, I heard all the statistics about what could happen to single-parent kids. My children had been through some hard places, but I had verses in my Bible that got dirty from me dragging my finger across them in prayer. I called one of them my lemonade-from-lemons verse: "Instead of the thornbush will grow the pine tree, and instead of briers the myrtle will grow. This will be for the LORD's renown, for an everlasting sign, which will not be destroyed" (Isaiah 55:13).

I had to pray this verse often when the past would appear to catch up with us. Once when Clint was about nine, he got very angry with one of his sisters. "I just inherited a bad temper," he said.

"Oh, no you don't," I said. I sat down with him and told him how he could accept the lie of curses or claim the truth of God's blessings on our lives. We prayed for him never to have a problem with his temper ever again.

At the age of thirteen, Clint came to me one day with a challenge. He had to write a paper about the last time he'd lost his temper for one of the classes at his Christian school. "Help, Mom," he said. "I can't remember the last time."

Together we looked back on God's blessings and His ability to reverse the curse.

Bible Study

Instead of a thornbush growing from the Samaritan woman's past, Jesus grew a pine tree. Instead of briers, He caused the myrtle to grow, both for the woman and those she told about Christ. All because Jesus got to the woman with the truth and switched her paradigm. He touched her. She touched others and brought them to Jesus. Then He began a work in their lives. This encounter in Samaria brought freedom to all who dared to come to Jesus, and it would never have happened if the woman had continued to dwell on the past.

About leaving your own water jar behind . . .

How do you feel today in the following areas:

Sense of worth from your childhood?

Sense of belonging from your adolescence?

Sense of competence from your adulthood?

What does God tells us to do to find freedom from the past?

Discover strength in Christ. Philippians 4:13: "I can do ____________ through him who gives me ____________."

Forget the past, look forward to the future. Philippians 3:13–14: "Forgetting what is _____ and straining toward what is __________, I press on toward the ___________ to win the prize for which God has called me heavenward in Christ Jesus."

Seek the bigger picture. 2 Corinthians 4:17–18: "For our light and momentary troubles are achieving for us an _________ _________ that far outweighs them all. So we fix our eyes not on what is seen, but on what is unseen. For what is seen is _____________, but what is unseen is ___________."

Become new. 2 Corinthians 5:17: "Therefore, if anyone is in Christ, he is a new __________; the _________ has gone, the ____ has come!"

What about freedom from curses?

Once a man named Balak sought out a man named Balaam to get him to curse God's people. The story is found in Numbers chapters 22—24. Balaam reports back to Balak that it couldn't be done. God not only reverses curses; He adds blessings in their place.

NUMBERS 23:8, 10: "How can I curse those whom God has ______ ___________? How can I denounce those whom the LORD has ______ _____________? . . . Who can count the dust of Jacob?"

NUMBERS 23:19: "God is not a man, that he should ________, nor a son of man, that he should __________ his ___________. Does he speak and then not act? Does he promise and not fulfill? I have received a command to bless; he has blessed, and I cannot change it."

Memorize PROVERBS 26:2: "Like a fluttering sparrow or a darting swallow, an undeserved curse does not ____________ ______ ____________."

What can He accomplish through your past?

In you. James 1:2–4, 12: "Consider it pure joy, my brothers, whenever you face trials of many kinds, because you know that

the testing of your faith develops _______________.
Perseverance must finish its work so that you may be
________ and _________, not lacking ________. . . .
Blessed is the man who perseveres under trial, because when he has stood the test, he will receive the crown of life that God has promised to those who love him."

Through you. 2 Corinthians 2:14–16: "But thanks be to God, who always leads us in triumphal procession in Christ and through us spreads everywhere the ____________ of the ____________ of him. For we are to God the aroma of Christ among those who are being saved and those who are perishing. To the one we are the smell of death; to the other, the fragrance of life."

And do you ever again have to be in bondage to the past?

GALATIANS 5:1, 13: "It is for freedom that Christ has set us free. Stand firm, then, and do not let yourselves be ________ again by a yoke of _________. . . . You, my brothers, were called to be free. But do not use your freedom to _________ the sinful nature; rather, serve one another in love."

Dear God:

When You set me free, I'm free indeed. Is there anything else I need to let go of? My childhood and adolescence were difficult in many ways. And as a woman, I've faced challenges too. Yet Jesus came to change all that. He restored dignity to those who dared to trust in Him. At the same time, He taught us to be servants. Help me do that, God, as I look to You to make good out of the bad, lemonade out of lemons and cypress trees from thistles. In Jesus' name, amen.

CHAPTER 5

I Am Growing

Developing Character Through Your Story

"When I am weak, then I am strong."

—2 CORINTHIANS 12:10

"Red Rover, Red Rover. We dare Lynda over."

I heard these words often during recess throughout my elementary-school years. Two teams would line up facing each other with hands joined. Then someone would call a name from the other side, and that person would run and try to break through their line. If the individual succeeded, she could choose one person to take back with her to her own team. If not, she had to stay.

I remember the strategy I chose when I heard my name called. My eyes would search the opposing team and select the most vulnerable place in their line. Then, with all the speed, determination, and strength I could muster, I shot across the field and sliced between my victims. The best I remember, I won every time.

As Christian women, we often play Red Rover in our spiritual lives, overlooking the need for growth in our search for significance. When we confront the need to improve personal qualities, we usually survey our lines and respond in one of two ways. We may look around and decide we have too much to work on, and we give up and decide not to fix anything at all. Or, we compare ourselves to those in the world who wrestle with the "big sins," and we decide we're okay just the way we are. Either way, we don't grow, change, or get better. We accept, instead, mediocrity and complacency. We come to Christ, attend church, learn Christian lingo, and that's where we stay, month after month, year after year. Whether we're the player who only sees her weak links or the one who concentrates solely on her strengths, we get into trouble when the enemy breaks through. After all, he's a master at knowing where we're vulnerable, and a chain is only as strong as its weakest link.

God designed that we would surrender our lives to Him as newborn babies, and then we—the main characters of our life stories—would grow. I've seen parents stand their children up to door jambs periodically to see how they'd grown during the previous year, marking the changes with their names and the date. What if these parents saw no growth in their children? Or the parents who keep copious notes each week in their child's baby book, recording new accomplishments—rolled over, took first step, grew first tooth. What if God kept a similar book to record your growth since you came to faith? What would you find written there?

Paul describes the growth process for Christians in 1 Corinthians 3:2, "I gave you milk, not solid food, for you were not yet ready for it [as babies]." The struggle with not shoring up the weak links—or growing at the door jamb—existed then as well as now, for Paul goes on to say, "Indeed, you are still not ready [for the solid food]." The Corinthians didn't grow.

But God doesn't force growth on any of us. He asks, instead, that we become submissive, or meek, when it comes to His work in us. Henry Blackaby and Claude King write about Matthew 5:5, which says, "Blessed are the meek":

> In popular thinking, the term meek implies weakness. The word Jesus used had a different meaning. His picture of meekness is that of a stallion that has been brought into subjection to its master. Whereas it once fought against any attempt to bring it under control resisting direction with all its strength, now it yields its will to its master. The stallion has lost none of its strength or endurance. It has simply turned these over to the control of the master. Meekness is not submitting to everyone around us, it is taking our direction from God. (*Experiencing God*, Walker and Co., 1999)

A number of years ago, I showed Arabian horses in English pleasure classes. I rode a gray stallion named Zelotmer using a snaffle bit, which had a double rein. The smaller rein of the two lay on top of my pinkie finger. When I wanted to check to see if Zelotmer would respond to me in the ring as he should, I lifted my pinkie to move the small rein connected to the bit in his mouth. If his head responded by moving up and to attention, I knew I maintained control. If he didn't respond and merely kept moving forward, he'd taken over the lead.

In the same way the bit curbed and restrained the horse, God longs to curb and restrain you and me by retaining control of our lives—the weak links—from day to day. And His control brings about growth for us. When we fail to hand over the reins in any area, it can mean trouble. Refusal to surrender our weak links will retard and even inhibit our Christian growth and cost us a vibrant life in Christ.

Scripture

We read of three characters in the Bible who probably knew what it felt like to be the losing team in Red Rover when they insisted on retaining control of certain areas. Each had his act together in many ways, yet vulnerable places in their lines permitted the opponent to break through.

Solomon was one such man. He was the wisest man who ever lived and greatly called by God. "Solomon showed his love for the LORD by walking according to the statutes of his father David, *except* that he offered sacrifices and burned incense on the high places" (1 Kings 3:3, emphasis added). When Solomon failed to surrender this weakness to God, it proved to be his undoing, despite his great wisdom.

David, Solomon's father, was spoken of as a man after God's own heart (1 Samuel 13:14). Yet he failed to surrender to God his lust for a married woman. He gave in to that lust, and this sin affected not only his life, but the lives of generations to follow.

Samson was a miraculous gift to a barren mother. An angel appeared to her and said, "You are sterile and childless, but you are going to conceive and have a son. . . . set apart to God from birth, and he will begin the deliverance of Israel from the hands of the Philistines" (Judges 13:3, 5).

And he was. "He grew and the LORD blessed him, and the spirit of the LORD began to stir him while he was in Mahaneh Dan" (Judges 13:24–25). But Samson found a weakness for a Philistine woman, the land from which Samson was to deliver the Israelites, and he pursued her while ignoring his father's warnings (Judges 14:1–2). This decision cost Samson his strength and ultimately his life.

Then there was the rich young ruler who came to Jesus and asked, "Teacher, what good thing must I do to get eternal life?" (Matthew 19:16).

Jesus explained that he had to obey the commandments to receive eternal life.

At that point, I'm sure this Red-Rover-playing young ruler must have examined his line and seen all its strong junctures. He responded to Jesus, "All these have I kept."

But then he asked Jesus a question that I believe you and I should ask today: In spite of all the things I am doing right, "what do I still lack?" (Matthew 19:20).

Of course Jesus cut right to the important matters. He found the one thing—his wealth—that lay between this young man and his commitment to Christ. Jesus simply said, "If you want to be perfect, go, sell your possessions and give to the poor, and you will have treasure in heaven. Then come, follow me" (v. 21).

Jesus wanted this young man to wade into deeper waters with Him. He gave him the choice of playing with his commitment or getting rid of every encumbrance that prevented a closer walk of faith. He was asking the young man for a deliberate decision to exchange his possessions that would pass away for eternal service to the kingdom of God that would never pass away.

What decision did the man make? "When the young man heard this, he went away sad, because he had great wealth" (v. 22).

He walked away from Christ. He chose not to shore up the weak areas of his life.

Oswald Chambers writes about this rich young ruler:

> He had come to Jesus filled with fire of earnest desire, and the word of Jesus simply froze him; instead of producing an enthusiastic devotion, it produced a heart-breaking discouragement. The Lord will not go after you, He will not plead, but every time He meets you on that point, He will simply repeat, 'If you mean what you say, those are the conditions. Sell all you have. Turn it all over to me. Undress yourself before God everything that might be a possession until you are a mere conscious human being, and then give God that.

The rich young ruler might have felt that Jesus was picking on him, but for all of us, God disciplines those He loves (Proverbs 3:12). Elisabeth Elliot writes: "God loves and has only one purpose for us: holiness, which in His kingdom equals joy. Holiness is a priority for God. When we seek to be like Christ, we seek holiness." And that happens by strengthening the weak places.

What Do I Lack?

Have I failed to seek forgiveness toward the one who brought me harm? Do I share unkind words about those who believe differently than I? Am I falling short in the love department and long on impatience toward those who do not believe in Christ?

I believe that the battlefields are dotted with fellow Christians—great men and women of God—who failed to surrender their weak points to God, and it became their downfall. In the beginning of the Bible, God instructed Moses to destroy all the old inhabitants when he arrived in the promised land, or they would forever cause the Israelites problems (Numbers 33:55). Today that means that when we get to the place to which God is leading, don't let old sins remain. We can look to Joshua to find what happens when we don't expel those who formerly lived there. The Gibeonites tricked them into believing they weren't who they really were. Joshua and his men did not consult God, and they fell for the deception. So they ate with the old inhabitants of the land, and thus established a new covenant with the very ones they should have gotten rid of. And the Gibeonites remained trouble to them from that point on (Joshua 9).

Our lines won't be impenetrable unless each and every joint is secure. Since our weaknesses will never all go away, we must look to God daily to reinforce those lines. After all, we're constantly being attacked by people and circumstances that seek to defeat us. The only way to reinforce our lines is to present what we have before God. We lay out who we are and what we're facing. Then we listen and allow Him to fill us with wisdom and to reveal the weaknesses in our defenses. His words cause us to listen throughout the day to ways we aren't being quite honest with ourselves or others, or giving responses that don't show the long-suffering of Christ.

A few years ago, a mentor of mine challenged me to go to God for thirty days and ask Him to reveal personal weaknesses, one at a time. Then he told me to pray and work on each area until I felt a breakthrough, then ask for another. I did just that, and one morning as I prayed at church, God dealt with me about some ineffective responses I'd had toward my daughter's unsaved friends. He let me know that He loved them as much as He loved my own children. Yet in my panic, I sought to save only my children and to make the best decisions for them. I realized I hadn't even prayed that God would touch the other girls' lives.

Red Rover, Red Rover, we dare Lynda over. My tenacity, determination, and good eye have helped me to win many attacks through the years. But I will forever be struggling with my defenses. Sometimes I become defeated on my own lines without the opponent ever coming close.

Solomon and Samson failed to surrender their weak points before they did them in. David finally did surrender and found forgiveness, though he had to deal with the consequences of his actions for the rest of his life. The rich young ruler came to Jesus with the right intentions but lacked the resolve to turn everything loose and serve Christ unreservedly. Corrie ten Boom once said: "Hold everything in your fingers loosely. It hurts when God has to pry your fingers loose."

God wants a people who will stand firm and strong for Him and will go to any lengths to serve Him in greater ways. He wants the hearts of people who never feel like they've arrived; hearts that are moldable and ready to do His bidding, no matter what the cost.

"This one thing ye lack," say the words of God to us today.

APPLICATION

We all have our weak links. God made us that way to draw us to Himself. We read in 2 Corinthians 12:9–10: "I will boast all the more gladly about my weaknesses, so that Christ's power may rest on me. . . . For when I am weak, then I am strong."

In his book *Bells and Pomegranates* (Destiny Image Publishers, 1991), C. Paul Willis describes the way we should look at shoring up these weak links. He talks about the high priest, who in Old Testament times was the only one who could go into the Holy of Holies to intercede for the people before God. On the hem of his robe, this priest wore alternating bells and pomegranates (Exodus 28:31–35). Willis writes, "The pomegranates acted as pads between the row of gold bells that reflected the light of oil lamps, and the soft fiber of the fruits kept the bells from striking each other."

Willis goes on to compare our lives today with that of the priest back then. After all, we are the ones who can now go directly to God through His Son, Jesus Christ. And our "robes" should look much like the priest's of old: alternating gifts and fruits. In the Hebrew ritual, the gifts of the spirit were symbolized by bells hanging from the robe of the high priest. We find those gifts listed in 1 Corinthians 12:8–11: wisdom, knowledge, faith, healing, miraculous powers, prophecy, distinguishing spirits, tongues, or interpretation.

But the author also says that our gifts should be tempered with the alternating fruits of love, joy, peace, patience, kindness, goodness, faithfulness, gentleness, and self-control (Galatians 5:22). Why? So our gifts won't clang against one another. Paul says it better in 1 Corinthians 13:1–2: "If I speak in the tongues of men and of angels, but have not love, I am only a resounding gong or a clanging cymbal. If I have the gift . . . but have not love, I gain nothing."

I worked on a writing project one afternoon, while my children were with their dad. I would not pick them up until six o'clock that evening. I had prayed for God's anointing, and I got lost in what I felt he gave me to write. It flowed, and I kept writing until the last second before I had to leave. I stopped at the gas station on the way. I hadn't brought any cash or credit cards, so I took out my checkbook. "I'm sorry, madam, we can't take checks," the attendant said. "You'll have to go get some cash."

Irritated that the man wouldn't trust me to write a good check but would trust me to leave and come back with the money, I huffed out the door and drove to a nearby grocery store. At the only open cash register in the store, a raggedly dressed woman took her time counting out change from a small plastic bag. I tapped my foot impatiently as she kept counting. Finally, I got to the counter, wrote my check, got my cash, drove back to the station, and paid the attendant. Then I realized, I'd enjoyed my gifts all afternoon, but they weren't tempered with the fruits of the Spirit when I encountered strangers.

And the Weak Become Strong

I have found that when I face conflict or someone has let me down, it's an opportune time to grow the fruits. Blackaby and King write:

> Each Christian has an inner longing that only Christ's righteousness can satisfy. But we cannot be filled with righteousness if we

are filled with self. Throughout the Scriptures, God emphasizes that the one who longs for Him with all his heart will find him (John 29:13). Our selfishness will be replaced by the fruits of the spirit—love, joy, peace, patience, kindness, goodness, faithfulness, gentleness, and self-control (Galatians 5:22–23). The Spirit will make us to be like Christ.

Holy God does not give His righteousness to people indiscriminately. He gives it to those who know they cannot live without it. Our desire for personal righteousness must be powerful, all consuming, dominating everything we do. Pursuing righteousness means that we value the opinions of God far more than we treasure the opinions of people. Righteousness is not merely an absence of sin. It is allowing God to fill us with His holiness (Romans 6:11). It is being like Christ.

So what does developing God's righteousness through the fruits of the Spirit mean in your life?

Love. "Love is patient, love is kind. It does not envy, it does not boast, it is not proud. It is not rude, it is not self-seeking, it is not easily angered, it keeps no record of wrongs. Love does not delight in evil but rejoices with the truth. It always protects, always trusts, always hopes, always perseveres" (1 Corinthians 13:4–7). Hannah Hurnard, in *Hinds Feet on High Places,* writes, "Every circumstance in life, no matter how crooked and distorted and ugly it appears to be, if it is reacted to in love and forgiveness and obedience, [God's] will can be transformed" (Destiny Image Publishers, 1993). These words describe just a few of the attributes of love. I don't know about you, but I have far to go in developing this fruit.

Joy. Mother Teresa said, "Joy is the characteristic by which God uses us to remake the distressing into the desired, the discarded into the creative. Joy is prayer. Joy is strength. Joy is love. Joy is a net of love by which you can catch souls."

The Bible tells us in Psalm 16:11 that in His presence is fullness of joy. That joy comes through trust. My children don't worry that they won't have food to eat in the morning when they go to bed at night. They trust Dave and me to have it there when they need it, and joy follows.

Peace. We all want that peace that passes understanding (Philippians 4:7). And Psalm 29:11 tells us that God will bless his people with peace. Author Dorothy Harrison Pentecost defines peace as, "Full confidence that God is who He says He is and that He will keep every promise in His Word." Frederick Buechner says, "For Jesus, peace seems to have meant not the absence of struggle, but the presence of love." For me, it meant reassuring five-year-old Courtney, when she grew fearful an earthquake the newscasters predicted would come the following day. I told her we were okay if the earthquake did occur and we went to heaven, or if it didn't and we continued to enjoy God's presence on earth. We had nothing to fear, so we could go to sleep with peaceful hearts.

Patience. We read in Romans 5:3 that tribulation grows patience in us. We all encounter hardship, and we can't do anything about it when it comes. We just have to wait. Once a mentor in our Cincinnati church asked me how things were going during one of my holding patterns. "Okay," I said, "but I'm not hearing from God."

"Could be," he said, "because you're right where you need to be, and He doesn't have anything to say."

I was learning patience.

Kindness. "Add to your faith . . . brotherly kindness," says 2 Peter 1:5, 7 (KJV). My dad used to say that kindness is love in its working clothes. You can take it out at the grocery store or with the mailman, with a stranger or even your enemies. Kindness works like magic to people you extend it to, and who knows, they might even inquire about its supernatural source.

Goodness. The origin of our goodness is the goodness of God, as referred to in Psalm 23:6 and 27:13.

Once when Ashley was five, she didn't finish her dinner. As I nursed her baby brother, I told her she would have to go to bed and miss Bill Cosby if she didn't go downstairs and finish eating. She went to her room and climbed into bed, then suddenly three-year-old Courtney disappeared. She returned soon and said, "Ashwee, you tan go watch Bill Tosby now, toz I went down and ate your food." That childlike goodness parallels God's goodness. We have none without Him. But His goodness through us allows us to forgive those who do us wrong.

Faithfulness. We learned in chapter 3 that God is our husband, and we read of his faithfulness to us in Scriptures such as Psalm 36:5, 40:10, and 89:1.

One night when my children were about ten, eight, and six, we were driving home after attending an outdoor theater presentation. Satisfied with the fun night we'd had, I leaned my head against the headrest and listened to the slow, even breathing of my sleeping children. Then I began to talk quietly to God. I spoke to Him about why He didn't appear to be moving faster and answering my prayers.

Then, as if He sat and talked to me directly, I felt Him speak to my heart, asking about how I felt about certain people and challenges I faced. I answered through my prayer. Then my mind went back to how I'd felt a year before about those same people and crises, and I realized I had matured in my faith. During a time when it appeared that nothing was happening, *something* was happening. I was learning to be more like Christ.

Major Ian Thomas, president of Torchbearers ministry, says, "The Christian life is not spectacular, just miraculous." God's work in me and His interest in helping me grow were made apparent to me in my car that night. The realization was not spectacular to anyone, just miraculous to me.

Gentleness. I tried to catch an untamed cat once at my uncle's house. Every time it came near, I chased after it. If I'd only known to take good food to the cat and let it develop trust in me, I could have made that feline creature mine that summer. I hadn't yet learned about the gentleness of Christ referred to in 2 Corinthians 10:1.

Self-control. We've already seen how we can struggle with our value as a person as we navigate our way through life. When it comes to self-esteem, we can respond to how we feel we're perceived by others in one of several ways:

- APPROVAL—You attempt to please others at any cost and are overly sensitive to criticism. This causes you to maintain a pragmatic identity psychologists call self-monitoring. It means that you adapt your actions to fit the circumstances.
- PERFECTIONISM—You feel you need to do everything perfectly all the time, in your home, the bedroom, and the workplace.
- WITHDRAWAL—You avoid important people in order to avoid disapproval.
- GUILT—You base your self-worth on past failures, dissatisfaction with personal appearance, or bad habits. You feel unworthy of love and that you deserve to be punished.

- VICTIMIZATION—You feel your plight is someone else's fault.

Self-control allows us to not be ruled by our emotions. It also allows us to resist further strongholds and revise our stories as we discussed in chapter 2. In his book *A New Guide to Rational Living* (Prentice-Hall, 1975), Dr. Albert Ellis talks about the A-B-C model of emotional health. He calls "A" the activating event, "B" the belief system, and "C" the consequence. Ellis reminds us that we cannot control most of the activating events that happen to us, but we can control our belief system. That belief system—how we respond and the self-control we exercise—determines the consequence. We can look to God's Word for the truth regardless of how things appear.

I remember once feeling discouraged because of the way I'd been perceived in a particular circumstance. I sat in my bathroom with my back against the wall. I prayed for God's guidance and forgiveness for anything I'd done wrong. When I had done all I knew to do, I sang. I didn't feel like it and circumstances didn't warrant it, but still I sang a song of praise while God fought my battle for me. I had learned somewhere along the way that the most central issue in self-control is learning to trust in God.

CONCLUSION

After my dad found the Lord, when I was six months old, he dedicated his life to serving God. During his pastorate, he did a lot of one-on-one ministry with people in our church.

In March of 1988, my mom visited my sixty-eight-year-old dad in his hospital room, where he stayed while being treated for pancreatic cancer. That Thursday afternoon, Dad talked about a couple of people God had laid on his heart and how he'd prayed for them. He also mentioned some things God was dealing with him about in his own life. Later, when a nurse brought Dad's supper to him, Mom excused herself to go back to her hotel for the evening. She paused at the door, turned, and said, "I'll see you tomorrow, Ernie."

That was the last time Mom saw her husband alive. He died at seven o'clock that night, but God was still shoring up the weak places in my dad and building the inner man just hours before he died. Why? Because he was one servant who dared to ask, "God, what do I still lack?" One of his favorite, often-quoted verses was, "But I keep under my body, and bring it into subjection: lest that by any means, when I have preached to others, I myself should be a castaway" (1 Corinthians 9:27 KJV).

Quiet growth with God is not spectacular, just miraculous. What about yours?

Bible Study

How have you grown spiritually in the past six months?

Name three ways you have grown:

Name three more ways you would like to grow:

What about the fruits? Describe ways you want to change:

- love
- joy
- peace
- patience
- kindness
- goodness
- faithfulness
- gentleness
- self-control

Do you feel reasonably certain that most sins could never trip you up?

Peter did. When Jesus told the disciples that someone would betray Him, Peter said, "Even if all fall away on account of you, ___ ______ ______."

"I tell you the truth," Jesus answered, "This very night, before the rooster crows, _____ _______ ______ _______ three times" (Matthew 26:33–35).

We are all just a night away from denying God if we don't walk closely with Him.

Regarding your responses to others about your significance:

MATTHEW 11:28–30: "Come to me, all you who are _____ and ________, and I will give you _____. Take my _____ upon you and ______ from me, for I am _______ and humble in heart, and you will find rest for your souls. For my yoke is easy and my burden is light."

Memorize and respond to these Scriptures as you take on His easy yoke and light burden:

Approval. Galatians 1:10: "Am I now trying to win the approval of men, or of God?"

I will no longer ______________________________.

Perfectionism. Romans 3:23: "For all have sinned and fall short of the glory of God."

I will no longer ______________________________.

Withdrawal. Hebrews 10:25: "Let us not give up meeting together . . . but let us encourage one another."

I will no longer ______________________________.

Guilt. Romans 8:1–4: "Therefore, there is now no condemnation for those who are in Christ Jesus, because through Christ Jesus the law of the Spirit of life set me free from the law of sin and death. For what the law was powerless to do in that it was weakened by the sinful nature, God did by sending his own Son the likeness of sinful man to be a sin offering. And so he condemned sin in sinful man, in order that the righteous requirements of the law might be fully met in us, who do not live according to the sinful nature but according to the Spirit."

I will no longer ______________________________.

Victimization. Isaiah 54:17: "No weapon forged against you will prevail."

I will no longer ______________________________.

Regarding your growth and strengthening weak links:

"When he heard this, he became very sad, because he was a man of great wealth" (Luke 18:23). Are you rich in something, too, that stands between you and God?

ROMANS 12:1–2: "Offer your ______ as living

________, holy and pleasing to God—this is your spiritual act of worship. Do not _______ any longer to the pattern of this world, but be _________ by the renewing of your mind."

EPHESIANS 2:1, 4, 10: "You were dead in your _________ and sins. . . . But because of his great love for us, God, who is rich in mercy, made us alive with Christ. . . . For we are God's ___________________, created in Christ Jesus to do good _______, which God prepared in advance for us to do."

EPHESIANS 4:22–23: "You were taught, with regard to your former way of life, to put off your _____ _________, which is being corrupted by its deceitful desires; to be made _________ in the attitude of your minds; and to put on the new self, created to be like God in true righteousness and holiness."

PSALM 139:7: "Where can I go from your _______? Where can I flee from your _____________?"

JOHN 15:1–4: "I am the true vine, and my Father is the gardener. He cuts off every ___________ in me that bears no fruit, while every branch that does bear fruit he ____________________ so that it will be even more ___________. You are already clean because of the word I have spoken to you. Remain in me, and I will remain in you. No branch can bear fruit by itself; it must remain in the vine. Neither can you bear fruit unless you remain in me."

PROVERBS 15:31–32: "He who listens to a life-giving ___________ will be at home among the wise. He who ignores ______________ despises himself, but whoever heeds correction gains understanding."

PROVERBS 3:11–12: "My son, do not despise the LORD's discipline and do not resent his rebuke, because the LORD disciplines those he _____, as a _______ the _______ he delights in."

HEBREWS 12:1–3: "Let us throw off everything that ________ and the sin that so easily entangles, and let us run with ________________ the race marked out for us. Let us fix our eyes on Jesus, the author and ____________ of our faith, who for the joy set before him endured the cross, scorning its shame, and sat down at the right hand of the throne of God."

Dear God:

When I am weak, then I can be strong through You, so I give You my weak links today. Grow character in me. Help me not to overlook little things that stand between You and me, and help me not to be overwhelmed at all the things I need to change. I've watched many people who didn't give their weaknesses to You. It proved their undoing and gave an entry point for Satan to work. Send someone to help me be accountable in my spiritual growth and to show me how to give You the reins of my life. What do I lack? Show me something I lack. Grow new fruit in me beginning today. And now I make a promise to You that I will not stop growing until my last breath on earth. In the name of Jesus Christ, amen.

CHAPTER 6

I Am Forgiven and Forgiving

Plotting the Events of Your Story

"Forgive us our debts, as we also have forgiven our debtors."

—MATTHEW 6:12

Lacy was in her early forties when she married John, a childhood sweetheart. He, a prominent defense attorney and she, a well-known speaker, prepared to live happily ever after. He had no spiritual background. She had some, which she'd placed on the back burner. But marriage and the subsequent challenges it presented clarified the need for a solid relationship with Christ, so Lacy grew close to the Lord, and prayed for her husband. He eventually also accepted Christ.

One Saturday morning, Lacy and John sat in a restaurant finishing their breakfast. A couple neither of them knew approached them, and the woman said, "Hello, we're the Tiptons. You just finished defending and acquitting the murderer of our daughter."

John and Lacy looked at each other, unsure of what else they were about to hear. Then the woman continued.

"On the first day of the trial I wrote a note to my husband that said, 'that man's attorney needs Jesus.' And we've been praying for you ever since."

John and Lacy went on to become good friends with this couple. But how could a relationship develop between the parents of a murdered girl and the man responsible for setting her murderer free? Forgiveness. Pure and simple forgiveness. The Tiptons didn't have to pray for John. Their salvation didn't depend on them doing so, but their growth and freedom did. They could have remained in bondage to their hatred, as many Christians do, but they chose to forgive those who had wronged them, just as Jesus had forgiven them.

Every one of us can plot out the events or actions of our stories and find injustices that never should have happened. Some of these atrocities were negative turning points for us, and we came to believe we could never get past them. We grew angry at the ones who perpetrated the wrongs. We direct that anger at God, "How could You let this happen?" at others, "Why did you do this to me?" or at ourselves, "How could I have been so stupid?"

No matter how the anger emerges or toward whom we aim it—God, others, or self—the antidote is forgiveness. No matter if the person who hurt you is alive or dead, the antidote is forgiveness. No matter how big or little the pain that resulted, the antidote is forgiveness. "Forgiveness is the antiseptic for our emotional wounds," writes Floyd McClung, Jr., in *The Father Heart of God* (Harvest House, 1985).

God is the One who causes forgiveness to happen, but we're the ones who give Him permission to do His work. He does not force it. In *Putting Away Childish Things* (Light & Life Communications, 1999), David Seamands writes, "There is only one place we can put our guilt to find a true sense of forgiveness—on the back of the crucified Christ."

When you don't forgive, you agree to revisit the hurt somewhere down the line and recount what's been done. You allow your identity to be defined by the hurts you've experienced. You set yourself up for additional pain in other situations by expecting to be hurt again. You become defensive and pass on destructive words and actions to others. And the failure to forgive and let go of one bad relationship spills over into all the rest.

Most of the time, forgiveness doesn't happen all at once. In his classic book *Forgive and Forget* (Harper & Row, 1984), Lewis B. Smedes lists four stages in the forgiving process that can bring about the kind of reconciliation the Tiptons portrayed:

We hurt. Somebody causes you pain so deep and unfair that you cannot forget it.

We hate. You can't shake the memory of how much you were hurt, and you can't wish your enemy well. You want that person to suffer as you are suffering.

We heal. You are given "magic eyes" to see the person who hurt you in a new light. Your memory is healed, and you turn back the flow of pain and are free again.

We come together. You invite the person who hurt you back into your life. If he or she comes honestly, love can move you both toward a new and healed relationship. If he doesn't come back, you have to be healed alone.

When we finally forgive and leave the vengeance to God, we give Him free reign to work with the leftover pieces and put them back together with His plan in mind. Only God can take a right response and change the outcome of wrong deeds. Only God can work even the bad things for our good. Only God can bring significance and eternal meaning to our lives, but only when we choose to forgive and respond as He does.

Scripture

I once took an administration class, where I learned about a Program Evaluation Review Technique (PERT). First developed in 1958 by the U. S. Navy, PERT can be effective in planning any type of project, but it is especially well-suited for large, complex, and lengthy tasks. Many people feel anxious when they undertake a large project because they often find such projects vague, open-ended, and ill-defined—much like our life stories. They don't have a good idea of the amount of time the project will take, so they don't have a sense of control over their time.

PERT charts serve as information-gathering devices that can provide an accurate idea of the amount of time and steps necessary for a task, and allow you to see the end product in terms of the time and effort it will take to achieve it. The three main components of the PERT process are: listing the necessary events, making time estimates, and developing a PERT flow chart. If I were to draw a PERT chart for my son, Clint, to use while cleaning his room, it might look like this:

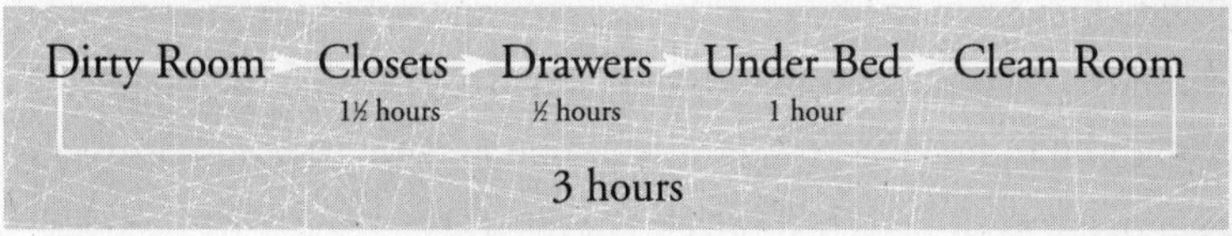

Dirty Room → Closets → Drawers → Under Bed → Clean Room
1½ hours ½ hours 1 hour
3 hours

Clint would not only know what he had to do to spruce up his surroundings, he'd also know how much time it would take to accomplish each task and finish the entire job—hopefully before he heads off to college.

One January, I took on the read-through-the-Bible-in-a-year project for the first time. I soon got to Joseph's story in Genesis 37, and I began to see a PERT chart emerge in his life story:

Home → Hole → Slavery → Prison → Governorship
13 years

Joseph starts out in a pretty normal way, the second youngest of twelve children born to his father, Jacob, in Canaan. Because Joseph and his younger brother were the sons of Jacob's favorite wife, they became his special children, and the other brothers were jealous of the favoritism their dad showed.

One day, seventeen-year-old Joseph tended the flocks near Shechem, a Canaanite and Israelite city in the hill country of Ephraim (later site of the covenant ceremony establishing the Israelite confederation in Joshua 24). Jacob had made a colorful coat for Joseph, and the young man had gotten a lot of attention for his elaborate dreams, so his brothers hated Joseph all the more. They decided to get rid of him. They threw him into a hole to die, but then the oldest brother decided they might as well make some money off of him. So they pulled him from the hole, stole his coat, and sold him to some traveling Ishmaelites. The Bible says in Genesis 37:28 that the Ishmaelites "took him to Egypt." I forgot this seemingly unimportant transportation detail until I reached the end of his story.

In Egypt, Joseph was sold to Potiphar, "one of Pharaoh's officials, the captain of the guard" (Genesis 39:1). Joseph found favor there, and Potiphar turned all kinds of duties over to his care. But Mrs. Potiphar got the hots for Joseph. She hustled him, and when he declined, she grabbed his coat as he fled and told Potiphar that Joseph had tried to rape her.

This made it a really bad year for coats for Joseph, and the woman's lie landed him in prison. While we don't know how much time passed between the individual events, the total time between Joseph's hole experience and his way out was about thirteen years—a long time to sit in prison thinking about the unfair things that had happened to him. He served God, and he might have asked, "Why did You let these things happen?" No one would have blamed Joseph for getting mad at his ten brothers or at the woman who had betrayed him. And Joseph might have even kicked *himself* for being so gullible.

Yet, in the balance of Joseph's life, we do not see evidence of bitterness. He hashed it out with God in the dungeon. He went through the hurt, hate, and healing stages right there in his cell. He chose to forgive, and though it took many years for him to be freed from a physical prison, he had long before broken free from the emotional prison that surely had him bound.

After a while, Joseph was pretty anxious to get out, as evidenced by his words to the cupbearer and the baker, who were thrown into prison with Joseph for offending their master. Joseph interpreted dreams for them in Genesis 40, and Joseph asked them to tell Pharaoh about him when they got out. But the baker died, and the cupbearer forgot all about Joseph (Genesis 40:23).

Two years later, the pharaoh had a dream too. The cupbearer told the pharaoh about his experience in prison. They brought Joseph to the palace, and he interpreted the pharaoh's dream. As a reward, the pharaoh made him second in command of Egypt and dream-interpreter point man for famine preparation. This time Joseph didn't lose a coat, but he gained one in Genesis 41:42, when the pharaoh dressed him in a coat of fine linen.

As governor of Egypt, Joseph saved God's people from famine by bringing his brothers, the tribes of Israel, into Egypt, and the coming-back-together part of the healing process began. Not only did the story turn out well for Joseph, but we see how God used the now thirty-year-old governor's forgiving responses to do a work in the history of mankind. This is how it happened.

The Bible says, "These are the names of the sons of Israel who entered Egypt with Jacob, each with his family" (Exodus 1:1). Scripture goes on to list eleven tribes. But where was Joseph? "Joseph was already in Egypt" (Exodus 1:5).

God had taken care of that important detail in Genesis 37:28, when the Ishmaelites delivered Joseph to Egypt. While things didn't seem to be making sense, they were making sense after all. He used the awful thing that Joseph's brothers did to bring glory to Himself. He used the rotten places and made history. But God couldn't have done it without Joseph's right response.

God used the hard-to-understand circumstances to accomplish His purpose in the end. Even Joseph recognized the meaning behind the trials when he said, "You intended to harm me, but God intended it for good to accomplish what is now being done, the saving of many lives" (Genesis 50:20). I call that verse the Old Testament version of Romans 8:28: "All things God works for the good of those who love him, who have been called according to his purpose."

Joseph did the forgiving, God did the redeeming.

You do the forgiving and offer right responses in the wrong places, and God will work it out for your good and for the good of eternity.

Application

My children's father left when I was pregnant with our youngest child. I immediately committed my life to Christ and walked with Him in the ensuing years. I thought I'd confessed all my sins, and even reconfessed some. But one hot July 1998 afternoon in Dallas I learned I hadn't.

I had gone to the Christian Booksellers Association convention to interview authors for my magazine. Bruce Wilkinson, president of Walk Thru the Bible Ministries, sat in the chair across the table for our four-o'clock appointment. I had become acquainted with him two years earlier at the same convention during another interview. We'd stayed in touch, and I humbly considered him a mentor.

Bruce smiled and asked me how I was doing. I told him, and I was sure he'd be impressed with how I'd grown in the Lord in the time since we last met. Instead he said, "God wants to minister to you today. You have unforgiveness in your heart toward your ex-husband." And he read to me the familiar passage of Scripture in Matthew 18:23–35. I listened.

> Therefore, the kingdom of heaven is like a king who wanted to settle accounts with his servants. As he began the settlement, a man who owed him ten thousand talents was brought to him. Since he was not able to pay, the master ordered that he and his wife and his children and all that he had be sold to repay the debt.
>
> The servant fell on his knees before him. "Be patient with me," he begged, "and I will pay back everything." The servant's master took pity on him, canceled the debt and let him go.
>
> But when that servant went out, he found one of his fellow servants who owed him a hundred denarii. He grabbed him and began to choke him. "Pay back what you owe me!" he demanded.
>
> His fellow servant fell to his knees and begged him, "Be patient with me, and I will pay you back."
>
> But he refused. Instead, he went off and had the man thrown into prison until he could pay the debt. When the other servants saw what had happened, they were greatly distressed and went and told their master everything that had happened.
>
> Then the master called the servant in. "You wicked servant," he said, "I canceled all that debt of yours because you begged me to. Shouldn't you have had mercy on your fellow servant just as I had on you?" In anger his master turned him over to the jailers until he should pay back all he owed.
>
> This is how my heavenly Father will treat each of you unless you forgive your brother from your heart.

Bruce then talked about forgiveness. He explained how few people know how to truly forgive. The king forgave a debt that would have been impossible to pay anyway. If the talents were made of gold it would be worth more than $57 million. If the talents were made of silver, they would have been worth more than $3 million. But when the servant couldn't turn around and forgive the $3,200 debt, the king turned him over to the tormentor. Bruce drew my attention to my own responses regarding my divorce: "This event shouldn't still have an emotional hold on you after thirteen years. If you haven't forgiven, you're tormented."

I knew Joseph's story well, and I knew he remained in prison for about the same amount of time, thirteen years. But he was free within his prison, because he had long before settled the issue of forgiveness. My life was changed that day by what Bruce had me do next:

Identify the infraction. I named everything I could think of that had been done to me through the divorce. With each issue I recalled, Bruce laid an item on the table—paper clip, tissue, pencil. I named some things I'd never verbalized before, and some experiences were so bad even Bruce gasped. I found this activity much different than merely reliving the wrongs done to me. Instead, I reached down deep inside and lifted out the hurts, then laid them out one by one.

Acknowledge the pain. Then I talked about how these issues made me feel. This brought sobs from places I didn't know I had. At this point I asked Bruce why this was only happening now. "What happened to all the times I've said, 'I choose to forgive.' And isn't forgiving an ongoing process. Don't I have to keep forgiving?"

Bruce's response was simple. "Your choosing told God you were ready. But you either forgive or you don't. Once you do, it's over, though you may encounter new infractions that you'll also need to forgive."

Forgive. Next Bruce had me pick up each item one by one and let it go. "I forgive ______ for ______," I said to each event. Sometimes Bruce would stop me and say, "You're not there yet on this one."

Throw it away. Once I'd forgiven every item, it was a done deal. I threw each item away, a visible reminder that I had forgiven.

Ask for forgiveness. Finally Bruce had me ask God to forgive me for failing to forgive. He also had me pray for God to reveal any more unsettled issues that remained.

In the months to come, I would need to remember that these issues were behind me. That afternoon freed me to move on, and it freed God to use my experiences to minister to others. I have worked with countless women since that time, helping them to forgive also. I never could have done that if I hadn't, like the Tiptons, chosen to forgive. I just wish, like Joseph, I'd done it sooner.

Conclusion

About a month after that forgiveness journey, my children's dad, now remarried, called to talk with the kids one Friday night. I told him they weren't home, then before he hung up, I told him I had something to say. I described the forgiveness process I'd gone through, and I asked him to forgive me for any wrong things I had done and for failing to forgive him. He accepted my words, but it was clear he had not changed.

My part was finished. I'd given a more powerful witness to him than ever before, but he still wasn't a safe person for me. I had hurt, then hated, and now healed, but I couldn't welcome him as a friend, because there can be no reconciliation without repentance. I'd done my part. It was up to God to do the rest.

Bible Study

Each of you is somewhere in your PERT. Your beginning point and many places in between are clear. But where you're headed and the sense that can be made of many of your tragedies is not so clear.

If you've received forgiveness for your own sins and asked God to help you forgive others, you can know that all things will work together for your good. Joseph didn't brag about the success of his PERT until the end of the story, when he looked back to see all that God had done and the sense He'd made from the senseless.

While your story has not ended yet, let's take some time to reflect on where you've come from and what God has done so far:

Draw your own PERT. ________ ________ ________ ________

Starting Point X X X Ending Point

Total Time=______________

(Be sure to include time elements too.)

At what points did you forgive?

Where has God made meaning out of the madness, or used wrong done for His good?

Memorize these scriptures and touch the end of your PERT when you recite them.

GENESIS 50:20: "You intended to ________ me, but God intended it for ____________ to accomplish what is now being done, the saving of many lives."

ROMANS 8:28: "All things God works for the ____________ of those who __________ _________, who have been called according to his purpose."

What was God's ultimate end?

GENESIS 50:20: " . . . to accomplish what is now ______ ____________, the saving of many ________."

ROMANS 8:28: " . . . according to his ________________."

Christ's death is the basis of God's forgiveness of you.

MATTHEW 26:28: "This is my _________ of the _____________, which is poured out for many for the forgiveness of sins."

JOHN 1:29: "Look, the Lamb of God, who takes away the sin of the __________!"

ACTS 5:31: "God exalted him to his own right hand as Prince and Savior that he might give ____________________ and ___________________ of sins to Israel."

EPHESIANS 1:7: "In him we have _________________ through his blood, the forgiveness of sins, in accordance with the riches of God's grace that he lavished on us with all _____________ and ___________________."

1 JOHN 2:2, 12: "He is the ______________ __________ for our sins, and not only for ours but also for the sins of the

whole world. . . . I write to you, dear children, because your sins have been forgiven on account of his name."

Your forgiveness for others

MATTHEW 6:14–15: "For if you forgive men when they sin against you, your heavenly Father ________ also forgive you. But if you do not forgive men their sins, your Father _____ _____ forgive your sins."

EPHESIANS 4:32: "Be kind and compassionate to one another, forgiving each other, just as in Christ ___________ ______________ __________."

COLOSSIANS 3:13–14: "______ with each other and forgive whatever _____________ you may have against one another. Forgive as the Lord forgave you. And over all these virtues put on ___________, which binds them all together in perfect unity."

Dear God:

Forgive us our debts, as we also have forgiven our debtors. My part is to forgive the debt, Your part is to make something good from the remains. I now see there are people in my life I haven't forgiven, and I no longer want to remain imprisoned by unforgiveness. Reveal to me unforgiveness against You, God, other people, and even myself. Today I want to let all of it go, never to be picked up again. And then someday, I'll be able to look back over everything and see Your plan. How You brought good from the bad and Your purpose from the pain. I surrender it all to You. In the name of Jesus Christ, amen.

CHAPTER 7

I Am Finding Intimacy

Discovering the Theme of Your Story

"The people that do know their God shall be strong, and do exploits."

—DANIEL 11:32 KJV

It was an August evening in 1952. Paul made his way down the street of a small town in southwestern Ohio. I can almost picture him with his hands shoved deep into the pockets of his gray work pants, his shoulders stooped beneath the weight he carried. His wife had died of cancer two years earlier, and his daughter, eighteen-year-old Joan, now lay dying of a rheumatic heart. She had been given an early Christmas holiday and an early graduation from high school, as they did not expect her to live more than a few weeks.

Suddenly Paul stopped. He heard a song filtering through the heavy air. He followed the sound to a vacant storefront and peaked into the windows. People stood singing with their hands lifted. Paul slipped into the back unnoticed and watched the strangers sing to a God he didn't know, about things he didn't understand. Their emotion captivated him. When they finished the song, the evangelist called people to the front for prayer. Paul had an idea.

He moved back out of the building as unnoticed as he had entered, and he drove home. He told his son and his two other daughters that he would take Joan to receive prayer. "Over my dead body," his oldest, Audrey, said. The doctor was also opposed, saying that moving Joan could mean sudden death.

But Paul found himself without options. He asked around and found that the evangelist would be preaching in a tent on Friday night. When the time arrived, Paul transported Joan in his car and carried her on pillows into the tent. His feet crushed the weeds and tall grass as he took uncertain steps to the front. Audrey followed close by, concerned about her sister's well-being. "Joan wore a tent dress," Audrey remembers, "and I could see the rise and fall of her heart through her clothes."

The evangelist prayed for Joan that Friday night, and Paul took her home, looking much the same as she did when she arrived. But Audrey recalls the miracle they saw the next Tuesday, when Joan woke up completely healed. Joan not only made it to Christmas that year, but to forty-six Christmases since in perfect health. Today she boasts of a dozen grandchildren and one great-grandchild.

The story is true and has the makings of an interview with Oprah, but the greater miracle came as a *result* of Joan's healing. Her whole family found Christ. Audrey, who before this had never heard the word "God" spoken in their home, said, "I wanted to get to know the One who would heal my little sister."

And she did. First her father, Paul, heard the song of the people who sang out of their passion for God. Then Audrey and her husband, Ernest, heard the song and sang it for their eight children. I was number two of those children and six months old when my aunt Joan received her healing. In the months and years that followed, my mother pored over the Word as she stirred pots on the stove. I remember hearing her in our pantry—the only place she could find to be alone—crying out in prayer to the God with whom she had fallen in love.

I often think of my mother when I listen to women with marital or other relationship problems describe their inability to be intimate with anyone, especially God. I grew up watching intimacy develop between my mother and God. That intimacy extended to other people, and she passed on those skills and the desire to me. God never wastes an experience. Instead, He uses it to promote the theme of our stories—intimacy with Him.

Earlier in this book you discovered how in your own life story you'll find spiritual warfare, which you're equipped to handle. You know that you are loved. You've learned how to be victorious over past chapters in your story. We've talked about how to grow character through conflicts in your story. You've even seen how today's events—good and bad—become part of an eternal story, when we learn to respond like Christ.

While on this journey to seek God-significance rather than self-significance, you can develop a personal, intimate relationship with God, though it doesn't happen automatically. It takes work. There are lots of people headed for heaven who haven't yet learned how to be intimate with God. But I've often said knowing Christ wouldn't be half the fun if God couldn't personalize His relationship with each of us. I'm amazed at people who omit this part in their search for significance. Even if you find personal and financial success, if you don't make your one-on-one walk with God a priority, you'll always feel an emptiness in your heart. And you will never find complete intimacy with another person until you learn how to be intimate with God.

Frederick Buechner describes how we try to suppress this longing for intimacy: "[Our] original shimmering self gets buried so deep we hardly live out of it at all . . . rather, we learn to live out of all the other selves which we are constantly putting on and taking off like coats and hats against the world's weather" *(Telling Secrets,* HarperSanFrancisco, 1991).

I call intimacy song. Connie Neal calls it dancing in the arms of God. She writes:

> Dancing in the arms of God is a relationship between you and God that is based on love and mutual respect. The two of you communicate in a close, intimate setting. He holds you, but his embrace is the embrace of a lover, not the restraint of an oppressor. As partners in this dance, God leads, and you let him, moving with the flow of his leading. You are not enveloped in God, losing your identity as a unique person; you are who you are, retaining your freedom and individuality at every turn. *(Dancing in the Arms of God,* Zondervan Publishing House, 1995)

Authors Brent Curtis and John Eldredge describe intimacy as "romance," in their book *Sacred Romance* (Thomas Nelson, 1997):

> In all of our hearts lies a longing for a Sacred Romance. It will not go away in spite of our efforts over the years to anesthetize or ignore its song, or attach it to a single person or endeavor. Philosophers call this Romance, this heart yearning set within us, the longing for transcendence; the desire to be part of something larger than ourselves, to be part of something out of the ordinary that is good. The deepest part of our heart longs to be bound together in some heroic purpose with others of like mind and spirit.

Because the nature of intimacy with God is as individual as the people who find it, the descriptions vary. Whether you call intimacy song or dance or romance or something altogether different, we all need intimacy with our Creator to make our lives complete. Intimacy is the single most stabilizing part of our God-significance. Once you develop intimacy with God, you find close fellowship with Someone who knows you and your circumstances even better than you do, and He knows how to make things right. I often think of this relationship like the Maypole we would play on during recess in elementary school. We could swing out wide, but we couldn't get too far away because the center pole kept us grounded. Though the way you feel about yourself can vary somewhat based on circumstances, finding intimacy with God won't let you get too far from the truth of your value in Him.

After all, the overarching theme of your story—the author's purpose for writing your story in the first place—comes from God, who has wooed you since you were a child, seeking intimate, satisfying fellowship with you. I remember sitting on a post by a gate behind our home and pretending, hearing something and someone call to me in the silence of the woods. Curtis and Eldredge say, "Jesus' desire was not just to engage the intellect but to capture the hearts." To find this kind of heart fellowship, we shouldn't concentrate so much on knowing self as knowing Jesus and saying along with Scripture, "That I may know him" (Philippians 3:10 KJV). To know here comes from the word *gnonai* and it means to become familiar "by experience."

> Romance has most often come to us in the form of two deep desires: the longing for adventure that requires something of us, and the desire for intimacy—to have someone truly know us for ourselves, while at the same time inviting us to know them in the naked and discovering the way lovers come to know each other on

the marriage bed. The emphasis is perhaps more on adventure for men and slightly more on intimacy for women. Yet, both desires are strong in us as men and women.

One day, my mom sat with us in our living room, holding Bible study with us and talking about this intimacy, this song/dance/romance she had found. She read and asked us to memorize from the Song of Songs 3:1–3:

> All night long on my bed
> I looked for the one my heart loves;
> I looked for him but did not find him.
> I will get up now and go about the city,
> through its streets and squares;
> I will search for the one my heart loves.
> So I looked for him but did not find him.
> The watchmen found me
> as they made their rounds in the city.
> "Have you seen the one my heart loves?"

As a young girl of ten, I listened from across the turquoise-linoleumed floor as my mother shared these verses with us. I watched her wipe the tears from her face as she reflected on the events that had endeared the words and the One about whom the words were written to her heart. I felt temporarily moved by her emotion, but then I stared out the window and bugged my younger brother. I hadn't yet found the intimacy with God my mother demonstrated that day, but eventually my opportunity came. And I would discover that whether song, dance, or romance, intimacy would only come by sitting at His feet.

Scripture

While writing my doctoral dissertation, I used ethnographic research to gather my findings. I went out into the culture, studied it, and wrote about what I observed. If I saw something happen only once in one location, I knew the event could likely be an anomaly. But if I saw similar responses in several different settings, I could usually count on what I'd seen as reliable data. The ability to see the same thing occur in several different settings is called *triangulation,* and we can see it in the story of Mary of Bethany.

Portrait No. 1

We meet her three times in Scripture, and each time her life exemplifies intimacy. Mary lived in Bethany with her sister, Martha, and her brother, Lazarus, about two miles southeast of Jerusalem on the eastern slope of Mount Olivet. Jesus became a family friend, and He often stayed with them when He passed through the city.

One afternoon, described in Luke 10:38–42, Jesus had come to visit them again. I can picture Him reclining in the La-Z-Boy with Mary sitting at His feet. He talked, she listened. He taught, she learned. The more time she spent with Him, the more she fell in love with Him.

Jesus also loved Mary's sister, Martha, and He longed for intimacy with her too. But the Bible says she became "distracted by all the preparations that had to be made" (Luke 10:40). Not gambling or being immoral. Distractions for Martha meant housework—cooking, laundry, cleaning. Even the good things drew her away from the feet of Christ where Mary had chosen to stay, despite what needed to be done.

We soon see the result. After being away from his feet for a just a short while, little problems became huge ordeals for Martha. "Sure could use some help in here," she might have said. I can almost see her temperature rising as she glances at Mary and Jesus engaged in relationship as she engaged in chores. But while Mary "sat at the Lord's feet listening to what he said" (v. 39), Martha "came to him" (v. 40). She approached him, stood above him, and didn't listen to what He had to say. Instead, Martha told Jesus to make Mary come help her in the kitchen—carve the turkey and load the dishwasher.

But Jesus said, "Martha, Martha, you are worried and bothered about so many things; but only a few things are necessary, really only one for Mary has chosen the good part, which shall not be taken away from her" (Luke 10:42 NASB).

Martha missed the intimacy that Mary had found with Jesus by sitting at His feet.

Portrait No. 2

That "good part" demonstrated itself the next time we see Mary in John 11, when Lazarus grew ill. His sisters sent word to Jesus about Lazarus's condition. Jesus assured them that Lazarus wouldn't die and that his sickness would be used to God's glory (John 11:4). Jesus stayed for two more days finishing the things He'd gone there to do, then He took His disciples with Him back to Bethany. On his arrival, they found that Lazarus had already been in the tomb for four days, and people had come to console Mary and Martha.

When Martha heard that Jesus was on His way, she went out to meet Him. "If you'd been here, he wouldn't be dead."

"Your brother will rise again," Jesus said.

But Martha, unable to understand the depths of Jesus' words, said, "Yeah, sure, in the resurrection."

Then she went to get Mary. "The Teacher is here. He's asking for you."

When Mary heard this, she got up quickly and went to Him, and some of the mourners followed. She fell at His feet, a familiar place to her. "If you'd been here, my brother would not have died," and she wept.

Mary could have masked her disappointment in Jesus, but she had cultivated a relationship in which she could tell Him anything. So she did. She cried, and He cried with her. He knew her and understood her pain.

Jesus went with Mary and the others to Lazarus's tomb. "Take away the stone," He said.

But Martha, still not tracking with Jesus, said, "You don't want to do that. Lazarus stinks by now."

Jesus prayed then said, "Lazarus, come out!" (11:43).

And Lazarus rose from the dead.

Portrait No. 3

The third time we meet Mary, she is once again troubled. Scripture doesn't tell us, but I imagine her in the marketplace or on the street hearing rumors that the chief priests planned to kill Jesus. They would surely wait until after the Feast of the Passover, as there would be a riot if they did something now.

As a woman, I put myself in her shoes as they made their way across the cobblestones of the street toward her home. When she walked inside, did memories come flooding back to her of all that Jesus had meant to her? Did she touch His chair and remember sitting at His feet? Did she look into Lazarus's bedroom and acknowledge her brother would not be alive had it not been for Jesus? Did she recall all the times He looked deeply into her eyes and understood her heart?

I think she did. Then she must have remembered that the greatest honor a commoner could bestow upon royalty is to anoint them. So Mary found the most valuable possession she owned, an alabaster box of pure nard. The contents were made from the roots and stems of a rare and expensive Himalayan aromatic herb used for perfume. Mary probably picked up the box, clutched it to her breast, and headed out the door.

She made her way to the home of Simon the leper, father of Judas Iscariot. The story picks up in John 12 at a dinner being given in Jesus' honor. Martha served once again. I wonder, did Mary take a breath before she leaned against the door to go inside? When she looked around, she saw the men reclining around the table. Among them sat Lazarus, whom Jesus had raised, and Simon, whom Jesus had healed. One can only imagine the conversation taking place around their out-of-body experiences.

Mary moved to Jesus. The Mark 14 version of the story tells us "she broke the jar and poured the perfume on his head." This meant that she broke the seal that kept the scent preserved, and she lavished it on her intimate friend Jesus. Then Mary poured the ointment on Jesus' feet and wiped them with her hair. "Stop!" Judas said. "The perfume could be sold and the money given to the poor. It's worth at least a year's wages."

No one else in the room saw a reason for expressing such lavish devotion to Jesus that day. The disciples even called it a waste. But Jesus commended her for disregarding economy, schedule, or popularity with others. He and Mary had something really special, and she'd found it at His feet. Jesus calmed Judas's outrage with His gentle words: "You will always have the poor among you, but you will not always have me" (John 12:8).

Over the next forty-eight hours, the scent of Mary's devotion to Jesus must have followed him through his trials before Pilate and Herod, and on to the cross at Calvary.

I wonder if Mary stood and looked at Jesus as He hung from the cross. He was more than a friend and a visitor. He was her Lord, the one who understood her and knew her through and through. How abandoned she must have felt as she saw Him hanging from the cross. Their talks would never be again. Or would they? Suddenly she remembered His words, "[You've] chosen the good part, which shall not be taken away from [you]."

At His Feet and Beyond

It wasn't family circumstances that created Mary's kind of intimacy with Jesus. As a child, my family designated an area of ground for a garden on the back part of our one-acre property. Our neighbors just grew grass on their land, but early in the spring, my dad would have a farmer plow and disk the ground. Then he would push long rows with his hand plow and drop seeds and small plants into the furrows before covering them with rich dirt. Throughout the subsequent months, he fertilized, hoed, weeded, watered, and harvested the produce that followed, and we enjoyed the food all winter long. Our neighbors, who also had plenty of land, could have also had a garden, but they didn't desire one and didn't do the work involved to make it one.

In the same way, Martha and Lazarus had opportunities for deep intimacy with Jesus. Martha saw Him just as much, and Lazarus even experienced being raised from the dead by Jesus. Yet we don't see evidence of undying devotion from them as we do with Mary. Martha and Lazarus had a relationship with Christ—even a supernatural one—but they didn't know intimacy. Intimacy doesn't just grow when ground becomes available, just as our garden didn't just grow when we had a little extra land. As the owner spends hours plowing and disking and planting and weeding and watering the soil, that's when intimacy grows.

I met Mary of Bethany shortly after my surrender to Christ. I experienced hard times, and I talked to God about it all, day in and day out. Slowly my tears came less frequently, and I even began to laugh again. One day while the kids played in the yard and I washed our van, I prayed, "I don't thank You for what I'm going through, but I do thank you for the chance I now have to read Your Word and pray."

With the sponge in one hand and the hose in the other, I heard Him speak to my heart: "You've chosen the good part." I continued to remember that verse all day. That night after I finished reading my Bible, I reached to turn off the light of my green ginger-jar lamp, and I heard it once more. I turned the light back on, opened my Bible to search for the source of the words, and then I found Mary.

When I met my husband, Dave Bjorklund, for the first time, I liked him. After talking and spending a lot of time with him, I loved him. After more time with him, I fell in love with him. I wanted to spend every available moment with him. Then we married, and I found an intimacy I'd never experienced with another person ever before.

In the same way, it's okay to just love God. Many do and stop there. But as Mary discovered, in-love-ness is also available to us as Christians. We just have to want it more than anything, then do the work involved to get it. So what does that work require?

Application

For her sixteenth birthday, Courtney received a gift from her friend Ann. It was a CD with all her favorite songs "burned" onto it. Courtney said, "Mom, I liked her present the most because it proved how well she knew me. She knew what I liked."

We all share Courtney's desire to be known, and intimacy with God allows that to happen. The word *ginosko* refers to a "knowing" connection between two individuals. The word indicates a relationship between the person knowing and the object known. What is known is of value or important to the one who knows. As a result, a relationship develops between the two.

I read a story recently about a woman who climbed a small mountain one day. As she did, her contact lens popped out of her eye. She searched for it to no avail, and then she prayed for God's help. On the way back down the mountain, she met someone coming up who asked, "Did any of you lose a contact lens? We just found an ant carrying it up the hill."

God knows us, and He works in mysterious ways to help us realize that. But just as God knows us, we can know Him too. We read in Daniel 11:32 a promise to those who find intimacy with God: "The people that do know their God shall be strong, and do exploits" (KJV).

The word for "know" in this verse is translated from the word *yada,* which means "life-giving intimacy." We find the same word in Genesis 4:1 (KJV) where Adam "knew" or *yada* Eve, "and she conceived, and bare Cain." Nothing short of knowing God will bring about intimacy, and nothing short of intimacy will allow you to be strong and do mighty exploits. And to know God, you need to regularly:

Spend time together. When you drive or soak in the tub or take your walk in the evening, invite Him to go with you. You'll feel Him draw close to you and soothe away the stress and cares of the day. "Come near to God and he will come near to you" (James 4:8). One day I realized that just as I needed to go into my clothes closet to get dressed for the day, I needed to go into my prayer closet each morning to get equipped for the day. He wanted to spend time with me as much as I wanted to spend time with Him. At that point I looked at Revelation 3:20 in a whole different way: "Here I am! I stand at the door and knock. If anyone hears my voice and opens the door, I will go in and eat with him, and he with me." To me that scripture means, *Lynda, wake up. Let's spend some time together over breakfast. You tell me what's on your heart, and I'll tell you what's on Mine.*

Read and memorize His Word. That's where you get your ammunition against the enemy. That's also where you read your love letters from God. Job and Jeremiah read and memorized the word many years ago, before it was bound in leather and had their names engraved on it. But they fell in love with God by reading His message to them: "I have treasured the words of His mouth more than my necessary food" (Job 23:12 NASB); and "When your words came, I ate them; they were my joy and my heart's delight" (Jeremiah 15:16).

I know what they meant. Sometimes early in the morning when I "eat" His love letters and direction to me through the Bible, the words take my breath away and my tears fall. He talks to me then. Just Him and me alone with His Word.

Talk with Him. One Wednesday I had a headache. I struggled through the dinner hour and got the children and one neighborhood girl loaded into the car for midweek children's church. On the way, I had to pull over when the pain became too great. At church, I dropped off the kids and pulled to a quiet corner of the parking lot. I leaned back against the headrest and prayed, "God, I need help. Please heal my head."

Before I could get out the words, my head had stopped aching. Suddenly I realized that earlier I hadn't even prayed for my pain. I'd suffered through it as one without hope, when all along He wanted me to talk with Him about it. "Ask and it will be given to you; seek and you will find; knock and the door will be opened to you. For everyone who asks receives; he who seeks finds; and to him who knocks, the door will be opened" (Matthew 7:7–8).

Listen to Him. As women, we like to talk. But we need to cultivate an ear to hear His leading too, and that comes through being quiet and listening. After all, we read in Psalm 32:8: "I will instruct you and teach you in the way you should go; I will counsel you and watch over you." Curtis and Eldredge tell us when that might happen: "Our inner story is most audible early in morning or middle of night when the inner editor that tells us how we should respond to the world has gone off duty. That's when our heart speaks to us of the story that is most deeply ours." Psalm 5:3 says, "In the morning, O LORD, you hear my voice; in the morning I lay my requests before you and wait in expectation."

It's about Him knowing us and us knowing Him: "I am the good shepherd; I know my sheep and my sheep know me—just as the Father knows me and I know the Father—and I lay down my life for the sheep. . . . My sheep listen to my voice; I know them, and they follow me" (John 10:14, 27).

CONCLUSION

A few years ago, I sat on my bed holding Bible study with my three children from the Song of Songs passage my mother had us memorize many years before. I repeated the words my mother had taught to me, then went on to recite verse 4 for my family:

> Scarcely had I passed them
> when I found the one my heart loves.
> I held him and would not let him go
> till I had brought him to my mother's house,
> to the room of the one who conceived me.

Instead of turquoise linoleum, my children listened on gray carpet and watched me wipe the tears from my cheeks as I thought about the events that had endeared the words and the One about whom the words were written to my heart. The children seemed temporarily moved by my emotion, but then they looked out the window and bugged one another. I realized at that moment that the words and the intimacy and the relationship that once belonged to my mother now belonged to me, and that one day they would belong to my children. And that will happen *only* by sitting at His feet.

BIBLE STUDY

God knows you . . .

1 CORINTHIANS 8:3: "But the man who ____________ God is known by __________."

2 TIMOTHY 2:19: "God's solid ________________ stands firm, sealed with this inscription: 'The Lord knows those who are his.'"

NAHUM 1:7 (AV): "The Lord is good, a _________ and ___________ in the day of trouble; He knows (recognizes, has knowledge of and understands) those who take _________ and ________ in Him."

. . . And He wants you to know Him too.

Set two goals in each area below to help you get to know Him more:

Spend time together:

Read and memorize His Word:

Talk with Him:

Listen to Him:

You can't have intimacy if you're not faithful to the one you love.

God is a jealous God, as indicated by this verse:

DEUTERONOMY 6:5: "Love the LORD your God with all your *heart* and with all your *soul* and with all your *strength*" (emphasis added).

In early Jewish times, leather boxes with Deuteronomy 6:4–9 printed inside, called phylacteries, were used to reinforce this truth. They wrapped the phylacteries around their necks to keep the words close to their hearts, around the forehead to remind them of the responsibility for their soul, and around the back of their hands to represent strength.

Once you find intimacy with God, you can find intimacy with other key people in your life.

Who are those people?

How have you found intimacy with this person difficult in the past?

What would you like to have God help you do?

Spiritually you discovered four ways for growing intimacy with God. Use similar steps for finding intimacy with other people as well. What can you do in each of the following areas to help you deepen your relationships?

Spending time together:

Reading and memorizing God's Word together:

Talking and praying together:

Listening to Him:

Dear God:

Your Word tells me that, "The people that do know their God shall be strong, and do exploits." You know me, now I want to know You in a greater way than ever before. Help me to remember that everything is designed by You to draw me to Yourself. Intimacy with You is the theme of my story. I want that song, that dance, that romance of intimacy to emanate from every part of my being to You and through You to other people. As I do my part spending time, reading Your Word, talking with You, and listening to what You have to say, show me the pathway to intimacy and to the strength and exploits it brings. In the name of Jesus Christ, amen.

CHAPTER 8

I Am Called

Discovering the Purpose of Your Story

"You did not choose me, but I chose you . . . to go and bear fruit."

—JOHN 15:16

I sat preparing lesson plans for the night class I would teach later that day as I waited for Clint to return home from morning kindergarten. I heard the door open, and soon I felt strong little arms hug me around my neck. I don't remember what we ate for lunch that day, but I do remember what happened later that afternoon.

Clint asked me to read to him from one of his Bible storybooks. We curled up together on our tan corduroy couch with the spring sun shining on our backs through the picture window. Clint selected the account of Hannah and Samuel. I read it to him then stopped. "Hannah and I have a lot in common," I said as I looked into my son's brown eyes. "We both prayed for sons, and God gave us the very best."

Then I pulled out my Bible and showed Clint how Hannah blessed Samuel with her prayers in 1 Samuel 1:10, and how he later found favor with God and men (2:26). But in chapter 3, verse 7, we read, "Now Samuel did not yet know the LORD."

I pointed to our fireplace and told Clint how at one time, that wall had been only a pile of bricks. Then someone with a skillful eye received those bricks—some broken, some cracked, some whole—and built them into a thing of beauty. "I've blessed you," I said to him, "and you've found favor with God and men. But it will be up to you to surrender your bricks to God. No one can do that for you."

"What does it sound like when Jesus talks to you?" Clint said.

I answered him the best I knew.

"Well," he continued, "The other night when I started to go to sleep, I heard someone call my name. I looked up and didn't see anybody. But I knew it was Jesus, 'cause He didn't talk to my ears, He talked to here," and he patted his chest.

Some time later I appeared on the Focus on the Family radio program, and I told Dr. Dobson about my son's experience. Clint listened to the broadcast and said to me, "Mom, you need to get that story right. That wasn't the first time I heard the voice—it was just the first time I knew who it was."

Clint recognized the call of God at age six. Many of us were older. Some of us have never heard that call, and we assume God can't use us. We question our value to the kingdom and conclude that we're not talented enough or what we do isn't important. But in his book *My Utmost for His Highest,* Oswald Chambers says that when we feel the most unworthy for God to use, that's when He most likes to use us.

> As long as you think there is something in you, He cannot choose you because you have ends of your own to serve; but if you have let Him bring you to the need of your self-sufficiency then He can choose you to go with Him to Jerusalem, and that will mean the fulfillment of purposes which He does not discuss with you.

But if we're armed, loved, victorious, and growing, we're prime candidates for God to use. He has a call for each of us; we just need to receive it. We read in Jeremiah 1:5, "Before I formed you in the womb I knew you, before you were born, I set you apart." Set apart from birth? Why shouldn't we reach out and accept the calling that belongs to us?

When Clint heard God call him, he, too, realized he'd been set apart for a specific purpose. Now a teenager, he's still not sure what all that involves, but he is certain that he has a purpose, and he's on a quest to discover and live out what that purpose is. Knowing that he is set apart stabilizes his feelings of significance, gives him a way to organize past chapters of his life, and allows him to look forward to future ones, whatever they may bring. He also knows for certain that his purpose will be made clear as he surrenders his bricks, one by one, to God.

We know the outcome of Samuel's story after he received his call. Clint's story is still in process, and so are yours and mine. Let's look at ten people in the Bible and examine their calls, responses, and results. We'll even take a look at the mistakes some of them made. But for all of them, we'll discover their God-given purpose, how God accomplished this purpose despite the imperfect vessels He chose to use, and what these examples might say to us.

Scripture

"To call" means different things in different contexts. To a sleepy teenager on Saturday morning, it can mean when mom arouses from sleep, awakens, proclaims, or utters loudly. Webster tell us that to a boatswain—a ship's officer, who has charge of the ship's sails, rigging, anchors, and cables—a call means "to summon his sailors to their duties." As we consider God's call to us, however, we will settle on the definition, "to name, select, appoint, or designate for office, duty, or employment."

God appoints each of us the duties and purpose for which we were created. He takes our giftings and experiences and desires and rolls them into His central purpose, when we give our lives to Him. What He does and how He does it is often quite different from what we envision, but when we surrender our bricks to Him, He can make great things. After all, God has used His people to do His work since the beginning of time.

ABRAHAM

Background. A wealthy man, Abraham lived with his barren wife in Haran.

Call. Genesis 12:1: "The Lord had said unto Abram, 'Leave your country, your people and your father's household and go to the land I will show you.'"

Response. Genesis 12:4–5: "So Abram left, as the LORD had told him; . . . He took his wife Sarai, his nephew Lot, all the possessions they had accumulated and the people they had acquired in Haran, and they set out for the land of Canaan, and they arrived there."

Results. Abraham became the father of the Jewish nation.

MOSES

Background. Moses was born Jewish and raised by the pharaoh's daughter. As an adult, he slew an Egyptian and fled to Midian, where he married Zipporah. He kept the flock of Jethro, his father-in-law and a priest in Midian. Moses led the flock to the back side of the desert.

Call. Exodus 3:2–4, 10: "There the angel of the LORD appeared to him in flames of fire from within a bush. Moses saw that though the bush was on fire it did not burn up. . . . God called to him from within the bush, 'Moses, Moses! . . . So now, go. I am sending you to Pharaoh to bring my people the Israelites out of Egypt.'"

Response. Exodus 3:4: "And Moses said, 'Here I am.'"

Exodus 3:13–14: "Moses said to God, 'Suppose I go to the Israelites and say to them, "The God of your fathers has sent me to you," and they ask me, "What is his name?" Then what shall I tell them?'

"God said to Moses, 'I AM WHO I AM.'"

But still Moses questioned eleven times:

Exodus 3:11: Who am I to do this big job?

Exodus 3:13: When they ask me who sent me, what shall I say?

Exodus 4:1: They won't believe me or do what I say. They'll say God didn't show me this.

Exodus 4:10: I can't talk well. I am slow of speech.

Exodus 4:13: Send someone else.

Exodus 5:22–23: I've kept my end of the bargain, but You haven't kept Yours.

Exodus 6:12: If the people won't listen to me, I know Pharaoh won't.

Exodus 6:30: I have faltering lips. Why should Pharaoh listen to me?

Exodus 17:4: What'll I do? They're ready to kill me.

Numbers 11:11: How can you lay the burden of this big job on me?

Numbers 11:21–22: How will you provide for all these people (600,000 of them)?

Result. Moses led the Israelites out of Egypt, through forty years in the wilderness and to the edge of the promised land.

JOSHUA

Background. Joshua was the son of Nun and served as Moses' assistant as they led the Israelites in the wilderness.

Call. Numbers 27:18, 20, 21: "So the LORD said to Moses, 'Take Joshua son of Nun, a man in whom is the spirit, and lay your hand on him. . . . Give him some of your authority so the whole Israelite community will obey him. . . . At his command he and the entire community of the Israelites will go out, and at his command they will come in."

Deuteronomy 3:28; 34:9: "'But commission Joshua, and encourage and strengthen him, for he will lead this people.' . . . Now Joshua son of Nun was filled with the spirit of wisdom because Moses had laid his hands on him. So the Israelites listened to him and did what the LORD had commanded Moses."

Response. Joshua 1:10: "So Joshua ordered the officers of the people . . ."

Result. Joshua led the Israelites into the promised land.

GIDEON

Background. Judges 6:11: "The angel of the LORD came and sat down under the oak in Ophrah that belonged to Joash the Abiezrite, where his son Gideon was threshing wheat in a winepress to hide it from the Midianites."

Call. Judges 6:12, 14, 16: "When the angel of the LORD appeared to Gideon, he said, 'The LORD is with you, mighty warrior. . . . Go in the strength you have and save Israel out of Midian's hand. Am I not sending you? . . . I will be with you, and you will strike down all the Midianites together.'"

Response. Asked questions, Judges 6:13: "If the LORD is with us, why has all this happened to us? Where are all his wonders that our fathers told us about?"

Made excuses, Judges 6:15: "How can I save Israel? My clan is the weakest in Manasseh, and I am the least in my family."

Demanded a sign, Judges 6:17–18: "If now I have found favor in your eyes, give me a sign that it is really you talking to me. Please do not go away until I come back and bring my offering and set it before you."

Obeyed, Judges 6:20, 22, 24: "And Gideon did so. . . . When Gideon realized that it was the angel of the LORD, he exclaimed, 'Ah, Sovereign LORD! I have seen the angel of the LORD face to face!' . . . So Gideon built an altar to the LORD there and called it 'The LORD is Peace.'"

Result. Gideon led Israel in victory over the Midianites.

DAVID

Background. David, the youngest of Jesse's eight sons, held the seemingly insignificant job of tending sheep when he was called. God sent Samuel to Jesse's home to anoint a new king of Israel, and he checked out the most likely candidates.

Call. 1 Samuel 16:11–13: "So he [Samuel] asked Jesse, 'Are these all the sons you have?'

"'There is still the youngest,' Jesse answered, 'but he is tending the sheep.'

"Samuel said, 'Send for him; we will not sit down until he arrives.'

"So he sent and had him brought in. He was ruddy, with a fine appearance and handsome features.

"Then the LORD said, 'Rise and anoint him; he is the one.'

"So Samuel took the horn of oil and anointed him in the presence of his brothers, and from that day on the Spirit of the LORD came upon David in power."

Response. David went back to the fields to tend to his sheep, his job for that time, and he did it well. It was there that God prepared him for the job that lay ahead.

Result. David became Israel's greatest and most-loved king. He wrote much of the book of Psalms and became part of the lineage of Christ.

ELISHA

Background. Elisha's predecessor, Elijah, hid under a Juniper tree as he fled from the wrath of Queen Jezebel. Discouraged and exhausted, Elijah poured out his complaints. An angel fed Elijah, and God said, "Anoint Elisha son of Shaphat from Abel Meholah to succeed you as prophet" (1 Kings 19:16).

Call. 1 Kings 19:19: "Elijah went up to him and threw his cloak around him."

Response. 1 Kings 19:20, 21: "Elisha then left his oxen and ran after Elijah. 'Let me kiss my father and mother good-by,' he said, 'and then I will come with you.'"

Result. Elisha followed Elijah. He received a double portion of Elijah's anointing and did a greater number of miracles than any other except Moses.

ISAIAH

Background. Son of Amoz who saw the needs of his time and culture. He bewailed Judah's wickedness and exhorted them to repent.

Call. Isaiah: 6:8, 9: "I heard the voice of the LORD saying, 'Whom shall I send? And who will go for us?' . . . He said, 'Go and tell this people . . .'"

Response. Isaiah 6:8: "And I said, 'Here I am. Send me!'"

Result. Isaiah was the greatest of the Old Testament prophets.

Mary

Background. Mary was young, unmarried, poor, and she came from the unimportant city of Nazareth in Galilee. Mary knew about God through the books of Moses, the Psalms, and the prophets' writings. She held a deep reverence for God because she knew what He had done in the history of her people.

Call. Luke 1:28, 30–33, 35: "[The angel Gabriel] went to her and said, 'Greetings, you who are highly favored! The Lord is with you. . . . You will be with child and give birth to a son, and you are to give him the name Jesus. He will be great and will be called the Son of the Most High. The Lord God will give him the throne of his father David, and he will reign over the house of Jacob forever; his kingdom will never end. . . . The Holy Spirit will come upon you, and the power of the Most High will overshadow you. So the holy one to be born will be called the Son of God.'"

Response. Luke 1:29, 34, 38: "Mary was greatly troubled at his words and wondered what kind of greeting this might be. . . . 'How will this be,' Mary asked the angel, 'since I am a virgin?' . . . 'I am the Lord's servant,' Mary answered. . . . May it be to me as you have said.'"

Result. Mary became the mother of Jesus, the Son of God.

Boy with Fishes and Loaves

Background. We read in John 6:1–13 the story of the unnamed boy who sat in the audience listening to Jesus speak.

Call. Jesus asked the boy to give all he had—three fishes and five loaves of bread to feed the five thousand men plus women and children attending that day.

Response. The boy gave all he had.

Result. Jesus stretched the boy's provision to feed the multitudes.

PAUL

Background. Paul persecuted the Jews. In Acts 9:1–2 we read, "Saul was still breathing out murderous threats against the Lord's disciples. He went to the high priest and asked him for letters to the synagogues in Damascus, so that if he found any there who belonged to the Way, whether men or women, he might take them as prisoners to Jerusalem."

Call. Acts 9:3–4: "As he neared Damascus on his journey, suddenly a light from heaven flashed around him. He fell to the ground and heard a voice say to him, 'Saul, Saul, why do you persecute me?'"

Response. Acts 9:5–6: "'Who are you, Lord?' Saul asked.

'I am Jesus, whom you are persecuting,' he replied. 'Now get up and go into the city, and you will be told what you must do.'"

Result. Paul ministered to the Gentiles and wrote much of the New Testament.

APPLICATION

A number of years ago, a new technology called call waiting swept across the country. By using it, you can choose whom you listen and talk to on the phone. If you're engaged in conversation with one person and you hear the beep, you can excuse yourself and check to see if the second caller is someone to whom you'd rather speak.

You and I can use call waiting with God. We tell Him we'll do anything He asks. But then something or someone comes along that distracts us, and we neglect even our conversations with God. Other times, we think we've realized that we're equipped, loved, victorious, and growing, then something happens to challenge our self-worth, and we hang up on the call altogether.

What can we learn about the call of God from these ten

people—Abraham, Moses, Joshua, Gideon, David, Elisha, Isaiah, Mary, Paul, and the boy with the fishes and loaves?

God calls to everyone, but only a few hear Him (Matthew 20:16 AV). Most people use call waiting. God didn't address the call in Isaiah 6:8 to anyone in particular when He said, "Who will go for us?" Others didn't hear the question. Isaiah did and responded, "I'll do it." That's the kind of servant God looks for. You can't hear His call to you if you aren't listening. You can't respond to His call if you hold out thinking you'll find a better offer. If you're preoccupied with other things, God will get a busy signal when He calls.

God calls different kinds of people to do different kinds of work. Abraham was rich, Gideon was poor; Moses was old, Jeremiah, David, and Samuel were young. Faith Willard is a sixty-seven-year-old widowed woman who lives in Forestdale, Massachusetts. God has called her to form a home in Bangladesh, India, for boys rescued from slavery. Sixteen-year-old Heather puts her love for basketball to use in inner city Colorado Springs to play—and witness—to kids on the street. Any age, socioeconomic status, education, gender, race—God can use it all.

Mary impressed no one with her youth, gender, or ancestry. But it was because of this lack of self-significance that God assigned to her perhaps the best-known example of God-significance in the Bible. Mary became a usable instrument because she could claim no worldly significance in and of herself. "May it be done to me as you have said." These words indicate complete surrender on Mary's part. She held nothing back. And the end result? Her son Jesus would utter nearly the same words in Gethsemane: "Not as I will, but as you will" (Matthew 26:39).

Time varies. David went back to the field to tend the flock for an unknown period of time after he received his call. Saul's conversion happened immediately. One moment he stormed up the road, determined to capture and imprison Christians; the next moment he was blind and being led like a child to Damascus, and into Christ's kingdom and the work God called him to do. Some of you have been plopped right down in your purpose so clearly that it has made your head spin. Others of us know some things about God's will for our lives, but we find ourselves waiting for the rest to come to pass.

God makes something of nothing. God sees us in our finished state. An angel described Gideon as a mighty warrior (mighty man of valor, KJV). These words appear to have been spoken in satire, because at this point, Gideon was anything but a mighty warrior. God's words reflected Gideon's potential only through divine enabling. Gideon could have read all the self-help books available and attended seminars on how to become a man of valor. But God knew His purpose clearly, and when Gideon chose to follow God, he chose his God-significance. None of us have to be talented enough for God to use. He just wants us to give Him all our bricks—the broken, cracked, and whole ones—so He can build the wall.

God uses mistakes. Paul's story continues to unfold in Acts 9. We read about a disciple in Damascus named Ananias who heard from God in a vision, telling him to go find Saul so God could start His work in him. Ananias questioned God's wisdom because of the awful things Saul had done. But God said, "Go! This man is my chosen instrument to carry my name before the Gentiles and their kings and before the people of Israel. I will show him how much he must suffer for my name" (Acts 9:15–16). It doesn't matter what you've done. God chooses us as instruments, then he uses us as surrendered vessels.

God calls people to work in ways that suit their personality and background. Paul, a Type-A personality so successful at persecuting Christians, God assigned to recruit new followers of Christ.

Moses' background enabled him to understand the plights of both Egyptians and Jews, so God sent him to deliver the Israelites from Egypt. God never wastes gifts and experience. Similar to throwing sugar and eggs and old bread together, God makes bread pudding out of those who offer what they have on hand.

God uses many things to get our attention. He used an angel with Gideon, a heavenly light with Paul, a burning bush with Moses. He has used hardship and disappointment in some of our lives. But God's call is not usually this spectacular. It is often just an expression of the nature within that requires relationship between our souls and God. Like a human being whom we love and know so well, we start to think alike and know what He knows. We wait for Him to open and close doors so we will know our way.

God considers our requests. God called Elisha to be a prophet, but Elisha asked God to give him a double portion of what Elijah had. As a result, Elisha became a prophet with a double portion.

During the summer of 1991, my family and I visited my mother in Arizona. I knew for sure some things God had asked me to do, but I also felt passions and dreams that were unfulfilled. One hot, dry evening, I took a walk and talked to God about my work. I told Him I'd do anything He wanted. Then I felt Him urge me to also tell Him what I would like to do. Careful not to put my own desires in front of His desires *for* me, I came boldly to the throne (Hebrews 4:16) as I would before my daddy (Galatians 4:6).

When Jesus asks us what we want—as He did in Mark 10:51 to blind Bartimaeus—Jesus wants us to answer according to *His* will. We read in Psalm 37:4 to "Delight yourself in the LORD and he will give you the desires of your heart." But we find that when we start delighting in Him, our delights become His desires, our will becomes His will, our purpose becomes His purpose. Our significance becomes God-significance. I told God that day that while I worked for Him, I'd like to write and be available for my children. Today He's placed me in work I never imagined, and I'm doing that work around taking my kids to their basketball games.

The call of God is only the beginning. Oswald Chambers says:

> To be separated unto the gospel means to hear the call of God. When man begins to hear the call, that only begins the agony worthy of the name. Ambitions nipped, desires quenched, outlooks extinguished—separated unto the gospel. It's a continuous process. Woe be to the one who tries to put his foot in another direction like Jonah when once the call has come to him.

Once you receive the call and do everything you know to stay in His will, get ready for the ride of your life.

He meets us where we are and doesn't ask for what we do not have. God met David on a hillside guarding sheep, Samuel on his bed, Paul on the road he traveled, and Moses on the back side of the desert. And God didn't ask for hamburger and French fries from the little boy with fishes and loaves. Don't ever be concerned that you won't be able to do what God calls you to. He'll meet you right where you are, and He knows exactly what's in your basket. You'll never know how many your portion will feed until you're willing to give it away.

The call varies. God made prophets, kings, and writers, and as we saw in chapter 1, none was greater than another. In her book *Holiness in Hidden Places* (Countryman, 1999), Joni Eareckson Tada writes: "In His eyes, there are no little people because there are no big people. We are all on the same playing field. We all start at square one. No one has it better than the other, or possesses unfair advantage." Just do the job God has given you to do.

A surrender to the call means devoting oneself to God. Oswald Chambers says, "The call of God is not to any particular service but to devotion to Jesus Christ. Service is the overflow of superabounding devotion. A saint is never consciously a saint. A saint is consciously dependent on God."

To serve God means offering a deliberate love gift that acknowledges the call of God, then serving Him in the ordinary ways of life out of devotion to Him. For me, on an ordinary-April-30-1992-during-lunch-day, serving Him meant leading my son in the sinner's prayer when he asked.

These things happen during the process of obedience to the everyday call. So often we work for God thinking that His call will come at some spectacular point. But the real call of God is concerned with the process. What we call the process, God calls the end. His purpose is that you and I depend on Him and on His power now. It doesn't begin when we become king. It starts in the shepherd's field, being obedient to the everyday things that God calls us to now, as we allow the Son of God to be manifested through us.

The call will cost you. It's easy to sashay through life without hearing and obeying the things God tells you to do. There's a cost to discipleship, and it often involves isolation and misunderstanding. But once you become aware of God's purpose for you life, you're never the same again and nothing else ever quite satisfies.

Mary, the most privileged among women, learned that her exceptional privilege went hand in hand with sacrifice. Moses had experienced this before her. Paul would after her. Mary had to sacrifice her reputation, when she, as yet unmarried, became pregnant. The law stated that if a Hebrew bride had betrayed her husband and was not a virgin at the time of their marriage, she should be stoned without pardon (Deuteronomy 22:20–21). Mary exchanged her favor in man's eyes for favor with God.

It is easier to serve God without a vision, and it's easier to work for God without a call because you're not bothered by what God requires. Once you receive a commission of Jesus Christ, however, you can no longer work for him halfheartedly. Paul was indifferent to any consideration other than fulfilling the ministry he had received. Never question whether you are of use. But always remember that you are not your own but His.

CONCLUSION

One day, nine-year-old Clint watched his older sister Courtney (who is just over six feet tall) play basketball. "Basketball is just another brick for Courtney," Clint said.

I didn't know what he meant at first. Then Clint looked at me with a sideways smile that immediately took me back to that special day we spent on the couch talking about God's call on Samuel's life—and his.

Indeed, Courtney's basketball was just another brick to be surrendered to Him into the grand scheme of His purpose. And who knows? As Courtney yields this area to God, He's the kind of King who will probably incorporate her love for the sport into His plan for her.

The call of God asks only for Courtney, and us, to be obedient today. To play our hearts out with surrender to God in our passions and gifts and opportunities. We don't need to think of what comes next, because what we call the training and preparation, God calls the end. If we have a further end in view, we may miss the call of God for the present. Obedience and surrender is the end. And you can do that now.

Bible Study

"Before I formed you in the womb I knew you, before you were born, I set you apart." God knows us and has a special calling for each of us. That gives us God-significance. So where do we begin to find placement within that calling?

God told Gideon, "Go in the strength you have and save Israel out of Midian's hand. Am I not sending you?" David went back and did what he'd been called to do then. That's what God wants you to do. He wants you to go in the strength you have for now and do the job in front of you today. He wants you to be faithful over a few things so He can put you in charge over many things (Matthew 25:21).

So when He looks down on the earth He has made and on the people He loves and sees how much they need Him, He still asks as He did in Isaiah's day, "Who will go for me?" Are you willing to answer as Isaiah did, "Here I am. Send me" (Isaiah 6:8)? For you it may mean provision for the five around your dinner table or five thousand in an auditorium. "Went forth." "Ran after." Said, "Send me." "What will you have me do?" Will you remain in the folds with the sheep or become a king? Will you go to the mission fields or support the ones who do?

God asks us to give all we have today and allow Him to make it into what He wants for tomorrow.

God's part

JOHN 15:16: "You did not choose me but I chose you and appointed you to _________ and __________ _________—fruit that will _________. Then the Father will give you whatever you ask in my name."

2 CORINTHIANS 3:5–6: "Not that we are ____________ to claim anything for ourselves, but our competence comes from _________. He has made us competent as ministers of a _____ _____—not of the letter but of the Spirit; for the letter kills, but the __________ gives life."

1 PETER 5:10: "And the God of all grace, who called you to his _________ __________ in Christ, after you have ________ a little while, will himself restore you and make you _________, ____________ and steadfast."

JOHN 20:21: "Jesus said, '_______ be with you! As the Father has sent me, I am ___________ you.'"

JEREMIAH 29:11: "'For I know the plans I have for you,' declares the LORD, 'plans to ____________ you and not to harm you, plans to give you _______ and a _______.'"

MATTHEW 20:16 (AV): " Many are called, but few _______."

Your part

Walk worthy. Ephesians 4:1–3: "I urge you to live a life worthy of the calling you have received. Be completely _____ and ______; be ________, bearing with one another in love. Make every effort to keep the unity of the Spirit though the bond of _________."

Give it all you've got. 1 Corinthians 9:16: "Woe to me if I do not _______ the gospel!"

Make it a priority. Philippians 3:8: "I consider everything a ________ compared to the surpassing greatness of ____________ Christ Jesus my Lord, for whose sake I have ________ ________ ____________. I consider them ____________, that I may gain Christ."

Be a witness. Matthew 5:16: "Let your light ___________ before men, that they may see your _______ _______ and _______ your Father in heaven."

Don't be ashamed. Romans 1:16: "I am not ashamed of the gospel, because it is the _____________ of God for the _____________ of everyone who ______________."

Hang in there. 2 Corinthians 4:1: "Therefore since through God's _____________ we have this ministry, we do not lose heart."

Deny self. Luke 9:23: "If anyone would come after me, he must deny himself and ____________ ____ ________ ____________ daily and follow me."

Follow Jesus. Matthew 4:19: "'Come, follow me,' Jesus said, 'and I will make you ___________ of ______.'"

Don't boast. 1 Corinthians 1:26–29: "Brothers, think of what you were when you were called. Not many of you were ___________ by human standards; not many were ___________; not many were of _________ _______. But God chose the __________ things of the world to shame the _________; God chose the __________ things of the world to shame the __________. He chose the ___________ things of this world and the _________ things—and the things that are not—to nullify the things that are, so that no one may boast before him."

Regarding your own story . . .

Background. What has happened to you that will impact the call of God in your life? (Remember your PERT.)

What gifts has God given you?

Call. You do have a call of God on your life. Describe the process of hearing that call.

What else would you like to do with your life's calling? Evangelize? Sing? Speak? Write? Other?

Response. Describe your journey—including strengths and weaknesses—of responding to the call.

What can you do better in responding to the call?

Result. What would you like to accomplish with your life?

What about your dreams?

We need to dream. Poet Langston Hughes wrote in his poem "Dreams": "Without dreams, life is a broken-winged bird that cannot fly." Proverbs 29:18 (KJV): "Where there is no vision [dream], the people ___________."

Our dreams are put there for a purpose. Habakkuk 2:3 (AV): "For the vision is yet for an appointed time and it hastens to the end; it will not deceive or disappoint. Though it tarry, wait for it, because it will surely come; it will not be behindhand on its appointed day."

Clarify your dreams. Habakkuk 2:2 (AV) says, "Write the vision and engrave it so plainly upon tablets that everyone who passes may [be able to] read [it easily and quickly] as he hastens by."

Describe your dreams and what you would like God to do with them.

Dear God:

I didn't choose You, but You chose me and appointed me to go and bear fruit. What a wondrous realization that is. I am so thankful I have heard Your call, and I promise I will never put Your call aside for something or someone I perceive to be more important. Help me be content in my specific calling without comparing myself to others. Help me be patient and never step ahead of Your leading. Use my gifts as well as my experiences and my mistakes. I surrender all my bricks to You today, as I begin my life-long journey of answering Your call. In the name of Jesus Christ, amen.

CHAPTER 9

I Am Passing It On

Impacting Other People's Stories

"Therefore go and make disciples of all nations, baptizing them in the name of the Father and of the Son and of the Holy Spirit, and teaching them to obey everything I have commanded you. And surely I am with you always, to the very end of the age."

—MATTHEW 28:19–20

My husband, Dave, boarded a plane to return home after a business trip to Minneapolis. He hadn't been sitting long when a man named Kevin took his place beside him. They chatted for the two-hour flight. Kevin was not a Christian, and Dave told him about his own walk of faith. Kevin asked questions and Dave answered. Before the plane touched down, Dave asked Kevin if he wanted to say the sinner's prayer. Kevin did. He prayed thirty-four thousand feet above the ground, and he walked off the plane a new man in Christ, while angels rejoiced in heaven over a new convert.

I had a magazine deadline to meet one day. I worked furiously all morning. At noontime, I decided to pick up a sandwich, so I ordered one from my favorite restaurant. A young man named Cameron had waited our table on several past occasions. He was interested in becoming a comedian, so I had told him I'd bring in a tape some time of a Christian comedian I knew. I grabbed the tape from my desk that day before I left to pick up my sandwich. As I walked through the door of the restaurant, I thought I might take a longer break and ask for a seat so I could give the tape to Cameron in person. I sat down with my honey-mustard chicken burger as he approached. Cameron joined me and talked about his life. I listened and invited him to accept Christ. And there, over cold French fries, Cameron prayed the prayer of salvation.

Neither the walk off the plane for Dave nor the trip back to my office seemed quite the same after what we'd witnessed. Two names—Kevin and Cameron—had been added to the Lamb's book of life (Revelation 21:27), and God used two imperfect, busy, otherwise insignificant people to accomplish this most important task. Whenever Dave or I or any other Christian is tempted to think our lives don't make a difference, we must remember God's plan for using us to pass on the faith.

As we saw in chapter 1, we live in a fallen world where things often don't go our way and everything works against our living a life of trust in God. None of us knows the Kevins and Camerons we've missed by simply being too preoccupied with our own schedules or issues. It's okay to ask "Who Am I?" But the reason we can answer that we are anything at all is because we are armed, loved, free, growing, forgiven, intimate, and called through Christ. Knowing all that, there comes a time when those truths are a given, and we move into service for others. We get past the tunnel vision of our everyday selfish concerns, and we look for the Kevins and Camerons we can reach with the gospel. Then someone needs to disciple them; to leave them as new Christians is like leaving a newborn in the hospital.

Dave called Kevin early the next week and sent him a Bible and a book that would assist his growth. In addition, Dave connected Kevin with people in his area for follow-through and to help him find a church. We've had him to our home for dinner, where he asked more questions about our Christian growth and practices. We recently met Kevin and his wife for dinner at a restaurant where further discipling took place, and Dave stays in constant touch with him.

I had our pastor pay a visit to Cameron. Some time later, I returned with a work colleague to the restaurant for another honey-mustard chicken burger, and I asked to be seated in Cameron's section. He said that day, "I laid awake last night thinking about how much my life has changed. I thought I was headed in this direction," he said as he drew with his finger on the table, "but since you introduced me to Christ, I think I'm going here."

These experiences make me think of one of my favorite words, *prosaic.* It means everyday, ordinary, and it might have been one of Jesus' favorite words too. After all, He used ordinary things to accomplish His work. He spit in the dirt to heal the blind man and borrowed a boy's lunch to feed the multitudes. Jesus used the commonplace to impact the eternal.

That's why He uses you and me, ordinary people, to carry out His work. Just before He went to heaven, Jesus commissioned us: "Therefore go and make disciples of all nations, baptizing them in the name of the Father and of the Son and of the Holy Spirit, and teaching them to obey everything I have commanded you. And surely I will be with you always, to the very end of the age" (Matthew 28:19–20).

I lost track of Cameron when he left the restaurant, but Kevin remains in our lives. The greatest expression of our love and gratitude to God comes when we set aside our own concerns and ask Him to use us in the lives of others.

Scripture

In Acts 1, Jesus had gone to heaven. His disciples must have panicked about what to do. He'd told them earlier in John 14:12 that they would do even greater works than He had done. But still I'm sure they couldn't imagine what that meant. Then He told them how: "You will receive power when the Holy Spirit comes on you; and you will be my witnesses in Jerusalem, and in all Judea and Samaria, and to the ends of the earth" (Acts 1:8).

Jesus' plan for expanding the gospel meant that believers would use their prosaic items and spread the good news to those closest first—in Jerusalem (locally), then Judea (nationally), then Samaria (internationally). Dorcas's story illustrates this rippled effect. In Acts 9, we read that Dorcas lived in Joppa, a port town along the Mediterranean Sea. Many of the men in that city worked as fishermen. Many of those men were lost at sea. As a result, many of the women were widows.

That's where Dorcas came in. Scholars believe she was a single woman, so she knew a lot of those widows and their needs. And God used that familiarity. In fact, she is the only woman named as a disciple in the Bible: "In Joppa there was a disciple named Tabitha (which, when translated, is Dorcas), who was always doing good and helping the poor" (Acts 9:36). How did a woman without means accomplish this? How did a woman—and an unmarried woman at that—put aside her questions of self-worth and work to further the call of Christ?

Dorcas devoted prosaic items—her needle and thread—to those around her every day. She sewed clothing for the widows. When she died and Peter was summoned from Lydda, he found a room lined with women wearing clothes she had made for them. Peter sent everyone out of the room and got down on his knees to pray. Then he turned toward the dead woman and told her to rise (Acts 9:40). Dorcas opened her eyes and sat up. Peter helped her stand, then he presented her to those who waited.

Word spread, so Dorcas's impact spread as well. "This became known all over Joppa, and many people believed in the Lord"

(Acts 9:42). Today, Dorcas societies exist all over the world, feeding and clothing millions of people, all because God used one otherwise-not-so-outstanding woman to accomplish great things.

Modern-Day Joppaites

What does Jesus' command to make disciples mean to us today? In *The Bridger Generation* (Broadman and Holman, 1997), Thom S. Rainer categorizes societal traits based on the year of birth in current generations:

Builders (1910–1946). These men and woman lived through two world wars and the Great Depression. They tended to become powerful and affluent with only minimal education.

Boomers (1946–1964). This group became the largest generation in American history. Raised by stay-at-home moms, we faced the 1960s counterculture, which endorsed an antiauthoritarian, self-centered, and materialistic society. As we tried to fulfill our needs, we dismantled the institutions that made our childhoods secure.

Busters (1965–1976). These men and woman are twice as likely to be children of divorce, be more pessimistic, and have fewer children.

Bridgers (1977–1994). One third of bridgers—our children—will live in single-parent homes. Violence, media saturation, disappearance of moral boundaries, and devaluation of life have become regular parts of our kids' lives. Is there hope for this lost generation?

The current condition of mankind comes as no surprise to God. He loves us just as much as he did those first-generation Christians. That's why He made provision to meet those conditions, and you and I are part of that. He still commands us to go and make disciples. Because of our experience and familiarity with the circumstances this generation faces, God can use us to minister to their needs.

All we need to do is surrender our lives and experiences to Him. He's the One who multiplies our efforts to affect another. We read, "For in it the righteousness of God is revealed from faith to faith" (Romans 1:17 NASB). In his exposition on the book of Romans (Wm. B. Eerdmans, 1982), Donald Grey Barnhouse talks about this passage and what it means:

> The righteousness of God is not revealed to the five senses of man but it is revealed from faith to faith. The Greek is very interesting—*ek pisteos eis pistin.* It is literally that the righteousness of God is revealed *out of faith and into faith.* God does not speak to you directly from heaven, but he comes out of the faith of one heart into the faith of another.

The church prior to Pentecost counted only a few hundred believers. We read in the book of Acts how that changed through scriptures such as:

2:41: "Those who accepted his [Peter's] message were baptized, and about three thousand were added to their number that day."

4:4: "But many who heard the message [of Peter and John] believed, and the number of men grew to about five thousand."

5:14: "More and more men and women believed in the Lord and were added to their number."

6:7: "So the word of God spread. The number of disciples in Jerusalem increased rapidly, and a large number of priests became obedient to the faith."

9:31: "Then the church throughout Judea, Galilee and Samaria enjoyed a time of peace. It was strengthened; and encouraged by the Holy Spirit, it grew in numbers, living in the fear of the Lord."

Three decades later, because of the impact of the faith-to-faith passing on of God's righteousness, scholars estimated the number of believers had grown by 22 percent. That rate of growth continued for three hundred years. By the fourth century A.D., when Constantine converted to Christianity, the number of disciples may have reached twelve million, one-tenth of the Roman Empire.

As God surveys the state of things, His plan for keeping the salvation message alive does not lie in a sophisticated computer. His plan is no more complicated, in fact, than to use ordinary people like you and me to spread the Good News. Nothing will prevail against world evangelism. God's church will emerge victorious regardless of how things look.

When I think that He captures every one of our tears and life questions and turns them into tools for reaching the lost, I get excited. Discipleship puts a different slant on pain and suffering in light of eternity. So go ahead. Thread your needle. Then watch what God creates with the materials of your life.

Application

Courtney recently came home in despair. She had once again shared her faith with one of her basketball teammates, and she wondered if she'd said the right things because the girl had still not accepted Christ. I watched visible relief spread across my daughter's face as I explained it was the Holy Spirit's job to work in people like her friend. We're just here to do His bidding, and He won't let us mess up.

God wants us to be active in sharing our faith (Philemon 6)—including on the basketball court—but we must always remember that, "No one can come to me unless the Father who sent me draws him" (John 6:44).

We read in James 1:5, however, that if we lack wisdom, we can ask and He'll give us a whole bunch of it. Whatever method you use to evangelize or disciple someone else, be sure to seek God's wisdom. The Holy Spirit will guide you and help you customize your approach to the individual like Jesus did. He recognized the basic personalities of the people He encountered then used techniques that appealed to them.

Expressives

To expressive John, Jesus reclined next to him at the Last Supper (John 13:23–25).

Characteristics. Involved, outgoing, enthusiastic, warm, opinionated, talkative, intuitive, emotional, friendly, imaginative, stimulating, impulsive, excitable, dramatic, vigorous, lacks tolerance for details.

Techniques. For expressives, establish rapport with them first, then present them with the gospel. Keep on track with the basics, allowing careful, limited experimentation as a reward for results. Let the expressive know that for all the good life has to offer, she doesn't have anything without Christ.

Amiables

To amiable Peter, Jesus fished with him and walked on the water (Luke 5:1–11; Matthew 14:22–36).

Characteristics. Good with people, overly committed, nonaggressive and nonconfrontational.

Techniques. Slow down the pace and volume as you build relationship with amiables through a warm, enthusiastic, and stimulating attitude. Work on one item at a time in detail, and avoid overwhelming her with too many tasks or ideas that need to change.

DRIVERS

To driver Nicodemus, a member of the Jewish ruling council who came to Jesus at night to find out more about Him, Jesus didn't play around with words. He simply told Nicodemus he had to be born again and gave him instructions on how to do that (John 3).

Characteristics. Results and time-management oriented, businesslike, confident, risky, and independent.

Techniques. Don't show a demonstrative, impulsive, or emotional side when sharing the gospel with drivers. Back up your enthusiasm with results to prove that your idea works. Honor the driver's time and limits by staying prompt and to the point. Provide choices for the driver where possible, and let her select the course of action to take.

ANALYTICALS

To the analytical Pharisees who held to the letter of the law and questioned why Jesus healed on the Sabbath, Jesus said, "The Sabbath was made for man, not man for the Sabbath" (Mark 2:27).

Characteristics. Problem solving, data gathering, thorough, conceptualizing, analytical, aloof.

Techniques. Talk facts, not opinions, to analyticals, and break your information into component parts, like showing diagrams. Back up your facts with proof from authoritative sources. Be quietly patient while they discover for themselves what you already know.

CONCLUSION

My children and I needed to set up the tables for the monthly meal at the soup kitchen our church sponsored. I drove down the interstate in Cincinnati wishing I'd had a little more time to sleep that Saturday morning, and I thought about my unsure work situation. Some writing and media opportunities seemed to tease me, but things didn't seem to be working in my favor at the time. Frustration had resulted.

Conversation abounded in the car, when suddenly from the right, I saw a man merging onto the interstate. Instead of pulling into the right lane, he sped out of control across the left three lanes toward the four-foot cement dividing wall. "Let's pray, kids."

We all knew what to do. We'd done it before. Immediately a chorus of prayers rose from our car. And then, like a miracle before us on that early morning, with few other people on the road, the man's car turned and straightened into the far inside lane.

My hands shook on the steering wheel as we continued toward our destination. The man exited the interstate in front of us. We came to a stoplight, where we needed to make a right turn toward the soup kitchen. As the man sat waiting, I pulled up beside him and motioned for him to roll down his window. When he did, I said, "We were praying for you back there."

The man, still visibly shaken, said, "Thank you."

I had to let him know how seriously we had taken his near miss.

"No, I mean we *really* touched God's throne for you."

The man watched a mom and her kids pull away in a dirty little white car. We didn't lead him to Christ, and we wouldn't be there to disciple him. But I know we were appointed to be at *that* place at *that* time to tell *that* man about Jesus.

The Bible says, "Preach the Word; be prepared in season and out of season; correct, rebuke and encourage—with great patience and careful instruction" (2 Timothy 4:2).

I didn't roll out of bed that morning free from my own concerns and say to God, "Okay, I'm ready to work for You today." Truthfully, I worried about lots of things, and I felt my life had little impact. I would rather have been making my mark in the world. Instead, I did what was right in front of me: I fixed a good breakfast for my children, prayed with them, and kept an appointment to help feed the homeless. "You will be my witnesses in Jerusalem [locally], and in all Judea [nationally] and Samaria [internationally], and to the ends of the earth" (Acts 1:8).

All God wants is for you and me to keep ourselves ready for Him to work through us, in season and out of season, good days and bad, when we feel like it and when we don't. What do we do? Whatever lies in front of us. What do we use? Whatever we hold in our hands—the prosaic items. Whom do we reach? Those closest to us. Then, when we lift Him up from the corner of the earth He puts us in for that moment, He will draw all men to Himself (John 12:32). That makes us God-significant!

Bible Study

Discipleship—teaching others to follow Christ—is not an option for the Christian, it's a command. Consider this verse: "And anyone who does not carry his cross and follow me cannot be my disciple" (Luke 14:27). You come to Christ, you learn more about Him, you follow His teachings, you become a discipler. It's as simple as telling others about what Jesus has done for you. How were things before you trusted? When did you come to trust? What has changed since you trusted? You tell them—lift Him up—and He does the drawing of these people to Himself. It's our job to lift; it's His job to draw. They in turn become disciplers and reach people with the gospel around them. Even now, Kevin is busy telling those he knows about the recent change in his life, as he also takes part in the multiplication process of the Great Commission.

Passing it on began in Old Testament times.

In Exodus 12:21–23, God told Moses to apply blood to the tops and sides of the doorframes of each Jewish household, so the destroyer would not get at them. Then God told him to pass it on. Exodus 12:26: "And when your ____________ ask you, 'What does this ceremony mean to you?' then _____ them . . ."

In Joshua 3:1–17, we read the story about how God rolled back the Jordan River so the Israelites could cross over on dry land. Then God instructed them that when they reached the other side, they should erect one stone for each of the twelve tribes as a memorial marker, " . . . to serve as a sign among you. In the future, when your _________ ask you, 'What do these stones mean?' _______ them . . ." (Joshua 4:6–7).

God's command since the beginning was that you and I pass it on to those around us—at home, work, grocery stores, banks, airplanes. Then when He is lifted up from the earth? "[I] will ________ all men to ___________" (John 12:32).

Who are we, anyway?

2 TIMOTHY 2:20–21: "In a large house there are articles not only of gold and silver, but also of wood and clay; some are for noble purposes and some for ignoble. If a man __________ himself from the latter, he will be an instrument for noble purposes, made __________, _______________ to the Master and ___________ to do any good work."

To prepare yourself for noble purposes, you need to ___________ yourself.

Remaining ready in season and out of season.

Evangelizing. Mark 16:15: "Go into all the world and preach the good news to all creation."

Bill Fey, director of Hope Ministries in Denver, developed a formula for evangelism in his pamphlet *How Can I Share My Faith Without An Argument?* Dave used that method when he led Kevin to Christ. It goes as follows:

- The Approach. Ask these questions one at a time and allow the listener to respond without your comment:
  1. Do you have any kind of spiritual belief?
  2. To you, who is Jesus?
  3. Do you think there is a heaven and a hell?
  4. If you died right now, where would you go?
  5. If what you believe were not true, would you want to know it?

- The Bible. Allow the person to read the following out loud:
  1. Romans 3:23
  2. Romans 6:23
  3. John 3:3
  4. John 14:6
  5. Romans 10:9–11
  6. Revelation 3:20

- The Close. Ask these questions, which repeat the content of the six verses above:
  1. Are you a sinner?
  2. Do you want forgiveness of sins?

3. Do you believe Jesus died on the cross for you and rose again?
4. Are you willing to surrender yourself to Christ?
5. Are you ready to invite Jesus into your heart and into your life?

(RBC Ministries, 1997)

Discipling. COLOSSIANS 2:6–7: "So then, just as you received Christ Jesus as Lord, continue to live in him, ________ and ________ up in him, strengthened in the faith as you were ________, and overflowing with thankfulness."

EPHESIANS 3:8–9: "Although I am less than the least of all God's people, this grace was given me: . . . to make plain to everyone the ____________ of this ___________, which for ages past was kept hidden in God, who created all things."

Handle discipleship much as you do in caring for a baby to help it grow:

PROTECT—LUKE 22:31–32: "Satan has asked to ________ you as wheat. But I have prayed for you . . . that your faith may not fail."

FEED—1 PETER 2:2–3: "Like newborn babies, crave pure ________ __________, so that by it you may grow up in your salvation, now that you have tasted that the Lord is good."

TRAIN—1 THESSALONIANS 2:11: "For you know that we dealt with each of you as a father deals with his own children."

ENCOURAGE—COLOSSIANS 2:2: "My purpose is that they may be _____________ in heart and __________ in love, so that they may have the full riches of complete __________, in order that they may know the ___________ of God, namely, Christ, in whom are hidden all the treasures of wisdom and knowledge."

FELLOWSHIP—1 THESSALONIANS 2:8: "We loved you so much that we were delighted to share with you not only the gospel of God but our lives as well, because you had become so dear to us."

Dear God:

Thank you for saving me. Now I must go and make disciples of all nations, baptizing them in the name of the Father and of the Son and of the Holy Spirit, and teaching them to obey everything You have commanded them. Help me to be ready in season and out of season to do the bidding of the Holy Spirit, which draws individuals to Himself. Help me to not be so preoccupied with other things that I miss opportunities for what lies in front of me today. Give me one person to evangelize and one to disciple this week. In the name of Jesus Christ, amen.

CHAPTER 10

I Am Significant

Anticipating the End of the Story

"Therefore keep watch,
because you do not know
the day or the hour."

—MATTHEW 25:13

The earthquake happened at midday on September 1, 1923 in Kanto, Japan. This area of the world, some fifty miles south of Tokyo, had grown accustomed to earthquakes. They had even built their homes from wood and paper materials that would withstand these inevitable disasters. But nothing could have prepared them for the earthquake that took place that day, registering 8.3 on the Richter scale. The earth shook for nearly five minutes, initially killing 100,000 people and reducing 300,000 buildings to rubble. An additional 30,000 people perished as fires broke out from the noontime lunch fires on their hibachis.

My children and I watched a documentary about this disaster one Saturday night. The commentator explained that a major earthquake occurs in this vicinity about every seventy years, and he mentioned nearby subsequent earthquakes in Tangshan, China that killed 242,000 in 1976, and one in Kobe, Japan that killed 5,000 people in 1995. "There are more coming," the announcer said. "It's not a question of if, it's a matter of when."

The man's words rang in my ears as I listened to how the schools prepare for future earthquakes by bolting down computers and triggering their propane gas supplies to switch off in tremors above 3.5. Then the commentator described activities in the schools to honor National Earthquake Appreciation Day on September 1. The children jumped and played as they took part in earthquake-like activities. They'd heard it all before, so the warnings had become merely a festival, a holiday, a simulation.

As I watched the program, I couldn't help but compare this event to Christ's return. As Christians, we've heard it all before. We've listened to stirring sermons and breathtaking songs, and radio and TV messages abound. So when we're reminded once more that Christ is coming back, that we need to be ready and we need to bring others along with us, we receive the news with a yawn. The warnings have become merely a festival, a holiday, a simulation.

Together in this book we've looked backward at our stories to where we've come from and forward to where we're going. Now it's time to look upward toward the resolution—the end of the story—where the main dramatic complications are worked out. Sometimes we live as though this is all there will ever be. But if we've accepted Christ, we're on our way to live forever with Him in a mansion He's been preparing for us all this time. That's reason to celebrate! That's reason for walking the high road. That's reason for significance. And it's not a question of if, it's a matter of when.

Scripture

After the TV special ended that Saturday night, I picked up my Bible to hold devotions with my kids. I read to them from Matthew 24:1–18. This passage takes place at Herod's Temple near the Mount of Olives. At 900 cubits square of white marble, with stones

94 feet long, 10 feet high, and 13 feet deep, the temple boasted as a wonder of the ancient world.

Scripture picks up after Jesus and the disciples had toured the temple. They walked outside, and the disciples commented on all they had seen. Perhaps they leaned on some of the 162 columns holding up the porches as they oohhed and aahhed the mighty structure. "'Do you see all these things?' [Jesus] asked. 'I tell you the truth, not one stone here will be left on another; every one will be thrown down'" (v. 2).

Imagine Jesus ripping the wind out of their sails with His words, then turning and walking up to the Mount of Olives, which offered the most commanding view of the temple. "Tell us," [the disciples] said, "when will this happen, and what will be the sign of your coming and of the end of the age?" (v. 3).

Jesus answered:

> You will hear of wars and rumors of wars, but see to it that you are not alarmed. Such things must happen, but the end is still to come. Nation will rise against nation, and kingdom against kingdom. There will be famines and earthquakes in various places. All these are the beginning of birth pains. . . . but he who stands firm to the end will be saved. And this gospel of the kingdom will be preached in the whole world as a testimony to all nations, and then the end will come. (Matthew 24:6–7, 13–14)

Jesus could have been reading the front page of today's paper with the words He spoke to His disciples. He reminded these men that as His followers, they lived for something more, something eternal, and the way they lived their lives on earth should reflect that great calling. He told them that when the time came to go to be with Him, they shouldn't " . . . take anything out of the house. Let no one in the field go back to get his cloak" (Matthew 24:17–18).

These men may have had trouble tracking with what Jesus said that day. But as a woman, I understand. I've given birth to three children. Every time the date for delivery drew near, I would pack my bags and leave them by the door. I knew that those bags held everything I would need and nothing more. Then I went about my day, doing what came next, but staying ready for my inevitable departure, when I would grab my bags and head out the door.

"Don't take anything out of the house. Let no one in the field go back to get his cloak." I'm reminded of this same principle each time I get onto an airplane. The flight attendant never forgets to remind us: "In case of an emergency, leave all your belongings behind." Jesus spoke these words passionately to His disciples because He knew that departure was inevitable for all of us. It wasn't a question of if, it was a matter of when.

I believe Jesus wanted to caution His followers to watch their "waits." By that I mean the time between coming to Christ and going to be with Him. He knew about the tendency for each man to pack the wrong things or never pack at all. He knew that as people, they'd always fight the urge to concentrate on nonessential things or the desire to run back to gather what didn't matter. He had told them earlier, "Do not take along any gold or silver or copper in your belts; take no bag for the journey, or extra tunic, or sandals or a staff" (Matthew 10:9–10). Because like the temple, it would all be gone.

When I travel to speak, I have a couple of dresses I love to take because they don't get wrinkled. I pack them, shake them, run a quick iron over them, and wear them. No hassle. I also live out of my suitcase at the places I visit. I don't move in because I know I'll be leaving soon. We should do the same with our stays here on earth. It's not our permanent home, after all.

In case of emergency, leave all your belongings behind.

So what are our belongings? What are our temples? What does this mean to us today?

How's Your Wait?

When my kids were young, I didn't have much trouble *getting* my kids ready to go places, but I did find it difficult *keeping* them ready. One year I made clown outfits for the girls at Halloween. I got Courtney dressed, makeup and all, then I went to work on Ashley. Meanwhile, Courtney rubbed one eye with the back of her hand. This sent the makeup straight down into her little eyes, which caused her to cry, which destroyed an hour of my work, which forced me to start over. If it wasn't makeup at Halloween, it was spilled grape juice or the jumping dog or a torn hem or a missing button—while they waited to go.

Many adults I know struggle in similar ways. Even when they've asked Christ into their hearts, they have trouble waiting well for Christ's return. In Matthew 25:1–8 we read about ten virgins who waited for the bridegroom. Jesus compares them to the kingdom of heaven. Five of these virgins took along the lamps they would need, but they forgot the oil to light them. The other five virgins took oil in jars along with their lamps. The bridegroom took a long time to get there, and all of the virgins grew tired, impatient, and distracted. But at midnight, the call rang out. "Here's the bridegroom! Come out to meet him!" (Matthew 25:6).

All of the ten virgins woke up. Since the foolish virgins didn't have any oil, they tried to borrow some from the wise virgins. But the wise virgins didn't have enough to share and advised those who had none to buy some from the vendors.

So they did. The foolish virgins came back at last fully prepared, but it was too late. The five wise virgins had grabbed their suitcases in the corner and gone with Him to the wedding banquet, and the door shut behind them. When the other virgins arrived, they tried to get into the door. But the bridegroom responded, "'I tell you the truth, I don't know you.' Therefore keep watch, because you do not know the day or the hour" (Matthew 25:12–13).

Application

To watch our own waits, we need to pack suitcases that are big enough to hold what we need, but small enough so we're not burdened with unnecessary baggage. We'll need our own salvation—clean, spotless, unwrinkled—and we'll need to pack it just right so the wrinkles won't return while we wait. What else do we need to do?

Settle the Significance Issue

We've taken a journey together in this book about significance—the importance or value assigned to a person or thing. We've discovered that eternal God-significance should replace our quest for temporal, fickle self-significance. We know that our worth and our entry into heaven is not earned (except for maybe massage therapists whose places may be secure and whose books may be already filled!). Since we know that works won't do it and God's grace is free, we can concentrate on the other areas we've discussed in this book while we wait. Don't let Satan ever allow you to question your worth again. It will keep you from moving on to more important things.

Stay Committed

I once heard the story of a young man who served faithfully as a house boy to three servicemen. His duties included washing, cleaning, and cooking. The three men, however, played practical jokes on this young man, who in turn worked even harder for them. Eventually the men started feeling guilty and agreed never to do it again.

"No more soap in shoes?" he asked.

"No more soap in shoes," they promised.

"No more buckets of water above door?" he asked.

"No more buckets of water above door," they promised.

"Good," he said. "Then no more spit in soup."

Like this young man, we often *appear* committed, when in reality we hold back. Sometimes this lack of commitment means we haven't truly sold out to Him. Other times we hang on to things we shouldn't. Still other times, we live with unforgiven sin that blocks our prayers and ministry effectiveness.

Only true, nonnegotiable commitment will keep us true for the long haul. The appointed day may be delayed an uncomfortably long time. But commitment causes us to wait well no matter what and do His bidding. To keep your commitment strong, check your:

Availability. Jesus searched and failed to find many who were committed to His cause. We read in Matthew 9 how Jesus went all over teaching, preaching, and healing the sick. The more He did, the more He saw that needed to be done. He felt compassion for those who hurt, and He looked for others to help Him do the work. "Then he said to his disciples, 'The harvest is plentiful but the workers are few. Ask the Lord of the harvest, therefore, to send out workers into his harvest field'" (Matthew 9:37–38).

One day, we came home to a field full of cut hay and a fast-approaching storm. We knew that the rain would ruin our crop, so we phoned everyone we could think of to come and help us bail. But we found no one available, and we ended up doing it alone and gathering all we could before the storm came. The harvest was truly plentiful, but the laborers were few.

Thought life. The Bible tells us in Philippians 4:8–9 to think about things that are true, noble, right, pure, lovely, admirable, excellent, and praiseworthy. Use these criteria as the filter for the things you use to fill your life. Don't get sidetracked by ungodly things.

Goals. Set a goal, such as reading through the New Testament. Once you reach that, go for another. Keep yourself reaching upward and outward in your faith.

Options. Your decision to follow Christ should be a settled issue. As a child, I watched a twenty-eight-year-old man named Don stand in the church my dad pastored after he'd suffered multiple serious heart attacks and say, "I'm ready to die for Christ."

I asked my dad about the man's words and his habit to fall away from the faith as his health improved. "Perhaps he's ready to die for Christ," my dad said, "but I wonder if he's ready to live for Him."

Focus

My friend and president of Generation Ministries, Tim Kimmel, has a roll-top desk in his study. On the left side of that desk he has a picture of the hospital where he was born. On the right, he has placed a picture of his burial plot. In between he displays a picture of his wife and children. While this arrangement may not be the most tasteful decoratively speaking, he uses it to keep him focused and to keep his priorities straight. When a task demands his attention, he asks himself if it is important enough to occupy a place with the other crucial people and events in his life. If not, he lets it go.

It's hard to stay focused on important things with so many other responsibilities and activities to distract us. But if we don't watch, we can get just as distracted as the world by the nonessentials and miss out on places God has called us to work. So how do we stay focused?

Memorize Scripture. This will help you be sure each decision you make lines up with biblical truth. Develop a program. Memorize the Word as you drive or walk or dry your hair. Make it a lovely part of your day. Then when the enemy tries to tell you a lie, you can counteract it with the truth—"the sword of the Spirit, which is the word of God" (Ephesians 6:17 KJV).

Ask yourself, does it have eternal value? Run everything you do through this grid. Will it matter years from now?

Learn to say no. As women, we have a hard time not trying to be all things to all people. My mom once told me, "Lynda, if a speaker drops dead, they get another speaker. If a mom drops dead, there is no substitute." We all need to learn to say no.

Remain Unencumbered

Jesus' warning reminded the disciples that the Temple would fall down, so not to lean too heavily on the 162 columns.

A missionary came to our church once. He talked of serving in three different locations. At each of those places, he bought a chess set—one in ivory, another in bamboo, and another in teakwood. When he moved to his fourth assignment, the church began a building project, which meant raising funds. He felt God impress him to give the first thousand dollars, and he said, "God, I'm a missionary, remember? I don't have anything of material value except my chess sets." But after God continued to deal with him, he sold all three of them and got exactly one thousand dollars.

Over time, different members of the congregation purchased back the sets and presented all three as gifts to the man. As he set a piece representing each of them on the podium, the missionary said,

"God really wanted my chess sets. Right? No, God really wanted me—all of me."

This man had learned his worth in God and to be committed, focused, and unencumbered. He'd learned to watch his wait. How can you do the same?

Get out of debt. There's nothing more rewarding than living within your means. When unpaid bills hang over your head, you can lie awake at night and worry during the day how you will make ends meet. Meanwhile, you still want more.

Begin by finding how to be content with what you have. Ask God to show you how. Study and memorize scriptures such as, "Godliness with contentment is great gain" (1 Timothy 6:6 KJV). Then start trimming down.

Don't take on too many responsibilities. Let go of things that hold you back. Could someone else lead the Girl Scout troop while you spend time with the Girl Scout living in your home? Ask God for His wisdom in this area. Remember, our biblical priorities consist of God, husband, children—and then all the other things.

Conclusion

Occupied or preoccupied? In my lifetime, I've known people who didn't watch their waits. One of them was a man who mentored my parents in their early walks with God and appeared to be a sold-out Christian. He became a household name in our family, but then my parents lost track of him until he resurfaced in 1978. The man was Jim Jones, who led a cult in Jonestown, Guyana and ended up killing some nine hundred people, including himself. I don't know all the theological issues involved, but I do know that Jim Jones didn't watch his wait.

My dad did. My children and I had gone back to Indiana for a visit. We planned lots to do during our stay, but my sister Sue suggested we visit Uncle Conley. I hesitated, but we did. Just the mention of his name brought back memories of Dad praying and fasting forty days for his salvation. My dad had died eleven years before, however, and he never saw his older brother become a Christian.

Inside his house, ninety-one-year-old Uncle Conley sat on the coffee table in front of Sue and me. Four of our children watched from another couch. Uncle Conley started talking about his ailments. He wiped a tear from his cheek with a shaking hand. "Are you able to talk to the Lord about these things?" I asked him.

"Oh, no," he said. "Me and the Lord ain't friends. I done too much."

"But what would you like for Him to do?" I said.

"Well," he said, "I'd like Him to forgive my sins ifn' He could."

"Then look up and tell Him," I said.

He looked up at the ceiling and said, "God, can You forgive my sins?" And I led my uncle in the sinner's prayer. He died the following December.

That day, my dad's prayers were answered while his two oldest daughters and four grandchildren looked on—eleven years after he had gone to be with the Lord. My dad watched his wait.

Bible Study

Jesus tells us to "Occupy till I come" (Luke 19:13 KJV), not to *preoccupy.*

Become a fellow hero of the faith.

Hebrews 11:8–16 tells how Abraham and others occupied and watched their waits:

11:8: "By faith Abraham, when called to go to a place he

would later receive as his inheritance, ___________ and ________, even though he did not know where he was going."

11:9: "By faith he made his home in the promised land like a ___________ in a foreign country; he lived in tents, as did Isaac and Jacob, who were heirs with him of the same ___________."

11:10: "For he was looking forward to the __________ with foundations, whose architect and builder is ___________."

11:13: "All these people were still living by faith when they died. They did not receive the things ______________; they only saw them and welcomed them from a __________. And they admitted that they were aliens and __________ on earth."

11:14: "People who say such things show that they are looking for a ____________ of their own."

11:15: "If they had been thinking of the country they had left, they would have had opportunity to ___________."

11:16: "Instead, they were longing for a better country—a ________ one. Therefore God is not ashamed to be called their God, for he has prepared a city for them."

These men knew that it wasn't a question of if, it was a matter of when, and they lived like it.

Don't get tired or discouraged and give up.

Hebrews 6:10–12: "God is not unjust; he will not forget your work and the love you have shown him as you have helped his people and continue to help them. We want each of you to show this same diligence to the very _________, in order to make your hope sure. We do not want you to become __________, but to imitate those who through faith and patience inherit what has been promised."

2 THESSALONIANS 3:13: "Never tire of doing what is ___________."

Anticipate the end of the story.

Fact. Jesus is coming back someday, and probably very soon. Yet because His trip back seems so delayed, I fear we as Christians have grown tired and distracted in our preoccupations. We must remember, we're just pilgrims passing through, and we need to occupy—not preoccupy—till He comes. Ask yourself:

- Have I settled the issue of my God-significance?
- Am I committed to Christ no matter what comes or goes? Do I see a city out there whose builder and maker is God? Am I occupying until He comes?
- Am I staying focused on the things that matter—the jobs God has called me to do, or am I distracted with things (houses, land, riches, education), emotions (anger, fear, worry), or sin (backbiting, gossip, unforgiveness)?
- Are my bags packed and waiting at the door, ready for a hasty departure, or do I plan to run back into my house and grab my coat and other belongings?

Clint was visiting his dad a few days before he started kindergarten. I talked to him by phone and he asked, "How many days till I come home?"

We talked about it for a few minutes. "Well, how many more dark times is that?" he said.

On the first day of kindergarten, I stood in our yard at the end of our cul-de-sac and watched as the school bus unloaded two pretty little girls and my little tow-headed boy. As his little legs stepped down off the bus, I saw a jacket go one way and a book bag go the other, and those legs started running. He moved as fast as he could down the street and jumped into the arms of his waiting mother. "Oh, I'm so glad to be home," he said.

At midnight the cry rang out! "Here's the bridegroom. Come out and meet Him." It may be two dark times or twenty or two hundred. But we need to be ready. We need to run with passion toward that city out there which hath foundations whose builder and maker is God. We need to watch our waits.

Dear God:

I've settled the issue of my salvation. Now help me keep my lamp full and my wick trimmed and ready till I go to be with You, though I don't know the day or the hour when that will happen. Thank You for helping me see that my significance comes only through You, so no one can ever take it away. When I'm tempted to wonder Who Am I? *I will remember I'm a child of the King who is armed, loved, free, growing, forgiven, intimate, called, and passing it on. And now, Lord, help me watch my wait. In the name of Jesus Christ, amen.*